LATIN AMERICAN POLITICAL, ECONOMIC AND SECURITY ISSUES

BOLIVIA

SOCIAL, ENVIRONMENTAL AND ECONOMIC ISSUES

GLEN MENDOZA
EDITOR

NOVINKA

New York

Library of Congress Cataloging-in-Publication Data

Names: Mendoza, Glen, editor.
Title: Bolivia: social, environmental and economic issues / editor, Glen Mendoza.
Description: Hauppauge, New York: Nova Science Publisher's, Inc., 2016. | Series: European political, economic, and security issues | Includes index.
Identifiers: LCCN 2016007436 (print) | LCCN 2016013535 (ebook) | ISBN 9781634848862 (softcover) | ISBN 9781634849074 (ebook) | ISBN 9781634849074 ()
Subjects: LCSH: Bolivia--Politics and government. | Bolivia--Social conditions. | Bolivia--Economic conditions.
Classification: LCC F3321 .B66 2016 (print) | LCC F3321 (ebook) | DDC 306.0984--dc23
LC record available at http://lccn.loc.gov/2016007436

Published by Nova Science Publishers, Inc. † New York

CONTENTS

PREFACE

Bolivia is known worldwide for the mineral wealth it produces. It is also renowned for being historically a complex multicultural and multiethnic society. This book studies the social, environmental and economic issues of Bolivia.

Chapter 1 – Bolivia known worldwide for mineral wealth it produces; it is also renowned for being historically a complex multicultural and multiethnic society. In Bolivia, there live many times and different ethnic groups, among which can be highlighted, today, the Aymara, Quechua and Guarani them. There are a significant number of "ethnic minorities", among which the Chiquitano. Just over 60% of the current population of the country considered indigenous, according to the census conducted in 2001. While there is a complex web of social categories (mestizos, cholos, etc.) taken into account in the analysis of demographic Bolivia and the setting of the number of indigenous societies of consensus lacks, the data collected showed at least 34 groups living in urban and rural areas in the early twenty-first century there. Such groups have had and have meaningful participation in the political life of the country, throughout history, marked in recent years by large and severe turbulences. The chapter will focus on the indigenous presence in Chiquitanía: how the governments of Bolivia independent treated the indigenous peoples in the indicated period (between the nineteenth and twentieth centuries).

Chapter 2 – This chapter deals with the construction of Bolivia's eastern border, shortly after independence, before the Empire of Brazil. Becoming an independent country in 1825, not only from Spain but also from the territorial claims of Lima and Buenos Aires, Bolivia only made its first treaty limits with Brazil in 1867, after several setbacks. Regardless, only diplomats nominated by their central governments did not do a treaty like this. Before that, the local population, such as indigenous groups, settlers from both sides, black slaves as well as local governments have developed strategies to intend face the border area, with different interests and influence in that. To government administrators, the important thing was to ensure the "ownership" of the given territory, to others, as settlers and African slaves, the frontier meant to change social conditions possibilities.

Chapter 3 – Bolivia is the first Plurinational State in the world, in which the State, constitutionally, assures the coexistence of different nations in a common area. The creation of this new Bolivian State addresses processes of mass mobilisation which structure the history of this country, and which after the neoliberal reforms of the end of the eighties and in the nineties, reached the tipping point of questioning the traditional policies. The election of the first indigenous president in 2005 replied to said process of questioning and set different challenges for this national society and at the same time for the global society. From this perspective the objective of this article is to reflect on the complexity of the tensions among which emerged from resource nationalism, decentralisation, as well as communitarian politics related to the Bolivian case. This work is structured in three parts. The first introductory part, presents the dynamic creation of the Plurinational State of Bolivia. The central part of the text is the second one, which analyses various elements: 1) the country's resource nationalism studied from the Latin-American and world context, characterising the tensions surrounding the institutionalisation of social movements and their grassroots struggles; 2) the regulation of the multilateral administration of the natural resources and the economic distribution of its profits, specifically in the case of the non-renewable, which were strategic in the preceding ten years; 3) the impacts of the resource prosperity on the state commitments of advancing in the construction of the new constitutional order refounded in 2009; and 4) the simultaneous challenges of the government Bolivian in the redistribution of wealth, poverty and inequality reduction, similarly in the advances in the climate change agenda. To close this second part, cases of decentralisation and of TIPNIS Park are briefly presented as examples of structural divisions between the State and the sectors of Bolivian society which tension is observed such as resolving the transition of extractivism on a large scale towards innovative means of sustainability. Finally, the last part of this chapter describes an environmental perspective which shows a contrast between capitalist production and the *Buen vivir* (well-being) models developed by the local Bolivian community, a fundamental contrast to understand the future of the Latin-American region. This contrast shows the fractures in the current urban capitalist modus vivendi and illustrates some communitarian practices, as alternative options to the global crisis.

Chapter 4 – Camelid populations are located at the Andean Plateau and produce essential incomes for native human population in Bolivia. Vicuna (*Vicugna vicugna*) is a wild endangered species which share territory and resources with other domestic camelids like alpaca (*Lama pacos*) in the National Apolobamba Integrated Area. Apolobamba is one of the poorest zones in La Paz Department. However, some natural resources such as the soil are much unknown. Further information is needed to determine their capacity to sustain the grazing activity in this area. The objectives of this survey were: a) to provide their edaphological classifications, b) to characterize the soil profiles in 8 zones with different vicuna and alpaca populations and c) to study their fertility based on physico-chemical properties. The investigation was conducted in Apolobamba Area, located in the Northwest of La Paz Department. Eight zones were selected taking into account the vicuna populations and the alpaca densities based on the last censuses data. One soil profile was identified in each zone and one sample was collected from each horizon. Two different key soil taxonomies were used to classify the soils. The most relevant physico-chemical soil properties were studied to characterize the soils and to determine the fertility. Six different types of soils were identified according to the soil classifications in the 8 studied zones. In general, soils presented medium-high organic carbon, total nitrogen, total phosphorus, cation exchange capacity and exchangeable cation contents. Moreover, the soils exhibited low electrical conductivity, acid pH, null equivalent calcium carbonate contents and different textures. Regarding to the soil fertility, the zones with higher vicuna and medium and low alpaca populations exhibited better fertility according to the soil properties studied in the profiles. Conversely, higher alpaca populations and lower vicuna populations were located in those soils with lower fertility (zones 1 and 3). Based on these results, higher alpaca concentration seemed to be associated to lower soil fertility while higher vicuna populations were located in soils with better fertility (zones 7 and 8). This observation points out the necessity to carry out conservation actions in order to preserve the soil fertility particularly in zone 1. However, these actions should consider that productions from both wild and domestic camelids are one of the most important economical activities in Apolobamba.

Chapter 5 – Artisanal and small-scale gold mining activities in Apolobamba area, northwest of La Paz, Bolivia, may produce serious environmental concern and great risk to human health. The current methods used to extract gold through the amalgamation process result in metal contamination of soil and water, as well as a negative effect on health of miners and inhabitants. Two main sources of contamination has been identified, the large amount of Hg used for gold extraction and the arsenic in the arsenopyrite from gold ores; also other metals, such as Zn, Pb, Cu and Cd, are associated to mining operations and may contribute to environmental pollution. The objectives of this work were to characterize the contamination of Hg, As, Cu, Cd, Pb and Zn in soils and sediments, and to assess the risk to human health and environment in different cooperatives mines in the highlands of Bolivia. In order to achieve these objectives, soils and sediments samples were collected, and physical-chemical properties and Hg, As, Pb, Cu, Zn and Cd analysed. Results showed that As and Hg concentrations were higher in top soils than in subsurface soils in the Sunchulli-Viscachani area, indicating active As/Hg atmospheric deposition, whose concentrations exceeded the soil Hg and As threshold levels. Oppositelly, concentrations of Cd and Zn largely exceed the thresholds levels in Katantika and Sural mining districts. These data indicated that a potential risk for human and environment could be taking place. In addition, Sunchullí and Viscachani lake sediments were contaminated by Hg, As, Cd, Zn and Cu, while Katantica lake showed high concentrations of Zn, Cd and Hg, and in the Sural lake were reported high levels of As, Zn and Cu. Results showed that Cu, Pb, As and Hg concentrations in sediments from the Sunchulli River; As, Hg and Cu in the Pelechuco River, and As and Hg in the Rayo Rojo River come from mine direct discharges into the rivers. These concentrations may cause a serious problem for aquatic life, related ecosystems and human health. Therefore, there is a need to study metals and metalloids availability and speciation in soils and sediments to better understand the cycling of these elements and transfer of metals/metalloids from soils into the food chain in the area.

In: Bolivia
Editor: Glen Mendoza

ISBN: 978-1-63484-886-2

Chapter 1

INDEPENDENT BOLIVIA: HISTORY, CULTURE, POLITICS, ECONOMICS AND INDIGENOUS TERRITORIES IN CHIQUITANIA IN THE 19TH AND 20TH CENTURIES

Giovani José da Silva*
Federal University of Amapá, Brazil

ABSTRACT

Bolivia known worldwide for mineral wealth it produces; it is also renowned for being historically a complex multicultural and multiethnic society. In Bolivia, there live many times and different ethnic groups, among which can be highlighted, today, the Aymara, Quechua and Guarani them. There are a significant number of "ethnic minorities," among which the Chiquitano. Just over 60% of the current population of the country considered indigenous, according to the census conducted in 2001. While there is a complex web of social categories (mestizos, cholos, etc.) taken into account in the analysis of demographic Bolivia and the setting of the number of indigenous societies of consensus lacks, the data collected showed at least 34 groups living in urban and rural areas in the early twenty-first century there. Such groups have had and

* Rod. Juscelino Kubitschek, KM 02 – Jardim Marco Zero Macapá – AP CEP 68.903-419 – Brazil. Email: giovanijsilva@hotmail.com.

have meaningful participation in the political life of the country, throughout history, marked in recent years by large and severe turbulences. The chapter will focus on the indigenous presence in Chiquitanía: how the governments of Bolivia independent treated the indigenous peoples in the indicated period (between the nineteenth and twentieth centuries).

Keywords: Bolivia, indigenous people, Chiquitania, 19th and 20th centuries

INTRODUCTION

Besides being known worldwide for the mineral wealth it produces, Bolivia is also renowned for historically being a complex multicultural and multiethnic society. In Bolivia, a diversity of ethnic groups have been coexisting for some time; principal among these today we can highlight the Aymara, Quechua, and Guarani. There are a significant number of "ethnic minorities," including the indigenous Chiquitano people who live in what is known as the tierras bajas. Just over 60% of the country's current population is considered indigenous, according to the 2001 census, despite the fact that researchers such as the Bolivian sociologist Silvia Rivera Cusicanqui have questioned the self-identification criteria used in this census (Rivera Cusicanqui 2008). Although there is a complex web of social categories (mestizos, cholos, etc.) to be taken into account in the demographic analysis of Bolivia, and despite the lack of consensus on the number of indigenous societies, the collected data showed at least 34 groups self-appointed as pueblos originarios living in urban and rural areas of Bolivia in the early twenty-first century (United Nations 2005).

Throughout history, these groups have had and continue to have significant participation in the political life of the country, which in recent years has been marked by great and severe turbulence as well as political innovations. Without slipping into any form of geographical determinism, a more accurate analysis of the country's terrain may help us understand this situation and clarify some important issues. Characterized by geographical discontinuities, Bolivia is basically divided into two clearly distinct regions: the Andean region or altiplano (mountainous, barren, cold, and rich in minerals) and the lowlands or tierras bajas (tropical climate, formed by vast plains, rich in oil and natural gas). According to the historian Leandro Mendes

Rocha (2006, p. 09) "in this latter region, which covers two-thirds of the country's, lives only a third of the population."

The tierras bajas cover the entire northern and eastern part of Bolivia and are divided into four regions: Yungas, Amazonia, Chaco, and Chiquitania. Yungas forms a transition zone between the Andean mountains and mountain ranges and Amazonia in the north of the country. Amazonia, in turn, consists of large expanses of rainforest which contain a great diversity of plant species. In the southern part of this region are broad plains covered with varieties of plants, which are used as pasture for large herds of cattle. The Chaco is an area of intense heat, covered by low forests, dry savannas, and some wetlands. Chiquitania, in the northwest (Department of Santa Cruz), is a less humid region and is covered by a landscape in which semi-wetland forest and savannas alternate. The tierras bajas have a total combined area of approximately 763,000 km^2 with vegetation covering 445,000 km^2 of this area (Birk 2000).

In addition to the geographical aspects, the competition from a variety of historical factors was instrumental in structuring the political, social, economic and cultural background of Bolivia, within an analysis, which cannot exclude past and present mobilizations of peasants and indigenous people, among others. [1] The importance of various historical events (including the 1809-1825 War of Independence, the Federal War of 1898-1899, and the 1952 Revolution) [2] refers to the way in which old and current internal processes are connected in this formation. It can be said, therefore, that the Bolivia of the twentieth and twenty-first centuries summarizes a history comprised of a heterogeneous ethnic, cultural, linguistic, and social mosaic; this mosaic contrasts with the political and territorial unity of the country, established in the early decades of the nineteenth century and mutilated by successive losses that totaled more than 1,000,000 km^2, the consequences of bloody wars and diplomatic treaties.

Between the second half of the 19th century and the first half of the 20th century, Bolivia suffered heavy military defeats to Brazil, Chile, and Paraguay; additionally, during this period it negotiated extensive areas of land with Brazil, Argentina, and Peru (Carvalho 2005). National and foreign

[1] According to the Brazilian sociologist Marcelo Grondin, "Between 1780 and 1783, the vice-kingdoms of Peru and La Plata [currently Bolivia] were the stage for the most significant indigenous rebellions in the entire history of the South American colony and which served as a prelude to the wars of independence" (Grondin 1984, p. 07).

[2] For more information about these events, please see Mesa; Gisbert; Mesa Gisbert 2007, among others.

interests were present during these events and caused or incited deep internal divisions among the Bolivian population. Not just material losses, but, above all, immense losses of life marked the involvement of Bolivians in such warring conflicts and diplomatic disputes. Although it has not been well-documented and has yet to be studied in detail, the participation of indigenous people in these conflicts is believed to have been intense, especially in the Chaco War (1932-1935) between Bolivia and Paraguay. Notable work in this direction include Jürgen Riester's efforts to recover indigenous Guarani narratives about the war (Riester 2005), as well as a recent study compiled by the French historian Nicolas Richard and originally published in Paraguay (Richard 2008).

The previously-mentioned ethnic and socio-cultural plurality constituted an ongoing challenge to the fragmented Bolivian society, as found by Herbert S. Klein (1994), and also requires researchers to pay extra attention to the complex relations established between the different socio-cultural universes. It should be emphasized that these relations were and still are strongly marked by a regional issue: those who live in the altiplano generally identify themselves and are identified as Collas (derived from Colla Suyo, one of the four old divisions of the Inca empire, which was also comprised of the Antesuyo, Contesuyo, and Chinchai Suyo, which together formed the Tawantisuyo, the "four lands"). But those who live in the tierras bajas generally are identified and identify themselves as Cambas. There is a historical rivalry between Collas and Cambas, which is often manifested in traditional regionalism.

Anthropologists and other investigators have observed that the use of terms, whether joking or serious, reveals cultivated biases for both the altiplano as well as the tierras bajas when these groups relate to each other. The Collas, for example, are said to have a predatory spirit, possibly inherited from the ancient Incan empire. As for the Cambas, it is said that they do not like heavy work, and as a result do not work much. So rejecting and discriminatory attitudes are culturally embedded and reproduced in everyday life not only within Bolivia, but also outside the country. And this does not even address the constant confrontation between the central government (partly based in the Andes in La Paz, associated with the Collas) and the Department of Santa Cruz de la Sierra (located on the plains and therefore associated with the Cambas), which often puts the interests of members of each group at odds (Montaño Aragón 1977; Hollweg 1977; Stearman 1987).

For the Brazilian anthropologist Sidney Antonio da Silva, however,

> [...] These two categories do not express the cultural diversity that characterizes these two regions of the country. [...] The Altiplano societies are characterized by agriculture, and consequently worship of the fertility of the land is common (Pachamama), while the tropical societies are characterized by livestock raising [...], the climatic factor also affected the way of being for men of the Altiplano and the tropics (Silva 1997, p. 73).

Of course, the issue of climatic influence on the lifestyle of human groups has been widely discussed in both anthropology as well as geography, since the use of these types or divisions can lead to the reification of stereotypes of all kinds. This does not mean taking such an influence as a determinant, but taking it into account and contextualizing it, confirming its reach case by case. In the case of Bolivia, it is possible to make correlations without slipping into determinism.

The German researcher Gudrun Birk, who lives in Bolivia, refers to these divisions as follows:

> [...], la composición étnica de los países latinoamericanos se diversificó y actualmente cada país tiene sus propias formas de nombrar y dividir a la población en grupos. En Bolivia, se hacen las siguientes distinciones:
>
> LOS COLLAS son los habitantes de la región andina, en oposición a LOS CAMBAS que son los mestizos del trópico.
>
> CAMPESINOS se llama a los quechuas y aymaras rurales de la región andina.
>
> COLONOS son los campesinos quechuas y aymaras que han migrado al trópico.
>
> INDÍGENAS es la autodenominación de las etnias del trópico y así son llamados por la población nacional.
>
> Cabe recalcar que la denominación "indio," que es utilizada en muchos países latinoamericanos para designar a los pueblos originarios, en Bolivia tiene una fuerte connotación racista y equivale a un insulto[3] (Birk 2000, p. 15).

---

[3] Translation: [...], the ethnic composition of Latin American countries has diversified, and now each country has its own ways of naming and dividing the population into groups. The following distinctions are made in Bolivia:

The COLLAS inhabit the Andean region, as opposed to the CAMBAS, who are the mestizos of the tropics.

CAMPESINOS are what the rural Quechua and Aymara of the Andean region are called.

COLONOS are the Quechua and Aymara peasants who migrated to the tropics.

As we have seen, such stereotypes, which are difficult to remove from various ethnographies, must first be questioned and relativized, and the Bolivian case is no different (Silva 1997, p. 74). This indigenous situation has not radically changed with the political independence of Bolivia, which occurred in the first half of the nineteenth century. If the Spanish Crown helped create and encouraged the differences between the strata of the Bolivian population, the Republic reinforced such differences, especially between the Spanish descendants (the criollos) and the mestizos and indigenous people from different ethnicities and origins.

THE FORMATION OF THE BOLIVIAN STATE AND THE INDIGENOUS PRESENCE IN CHIQUITANIA

As an independent Republic, since 1825 Bolivia has been politically comprised of the territory of the former Royal Audiencia of Charcas. Becoming a politically emancipated country in the first half of the nineteenth century and headed by Jose Antonio de Sucre and Casimiro Olañeta, Bolivia, in the words of Klein:

> [...] thereby was the most indigenous of the new republics in the Spanish Americas; a republic in which the tongue of the conquistadores remained a minority language until the twentieth century. Thus, the prosperous mining colonies of ages past emerged into a new Republican existence as an extremely poor society overwhelming composed of peasant Indians (Klein 1991, p. 73).

Throughout the colonial period until that time, what is now Bolivian lands was initially part of the Viceroyalty of Peru (1543), and later, when it was divided, the Viceroyalty of Prata (1776), with its capital in Buenos Aires. The Spanish conquest of this portion of the Americas followed the previous model of the conquest of Mexico and Central America, where an advanced military technology permitted hundred of Spaniards to overwhelm indigenous groups formed by thousands of men and women in a short period of time.

INDÍGENAS is what the tropical groups call themselves, and how they are referred to by the population of the country.

It should be emphasized that 'indian', which is used in many Latin American countries for indigenous peoples, has a strong racist connotation in Bolivia and is an insult.

Klein continues:

> Spain's kingdom in the Americas was organized into political-administrative units called viceroyalties. The first of these, the Viceroyalty of New Spain, was established in 1535; its capital was Mexico City, and it spanned Central America, the West Indies, and a considerable portion of the southern United States. In 1543, the Viceroyalty of Peru was created, with Lima as its capital. The Viceroyalty of Peru extended its jurisdiction throughout all of South America, which was under Spanish rule, including Alto Peru, which at that time was the name for the region which would form the base of most of Bolivia's lands, three centuries later (Klein 1991, p. 27).

Various groups populated Bolivia in the past, forming distinct and significant cultures: the Tiahuanaco, Mollo, Charcas, Urus and Chipaias, among countless others (Hany 2007). Before the arrival of the Spaniards, between the 12th century and the first decades of the 16th century an extremely complex society and state organization flourished in the southern Andean highlands, anchored in a dense system of farming villages. Around three million indigenous people were under the control of the Inca Empire, involving a multitude of different societies and speakers of many languages, which were grouped into a vast, non-market trade system. As for the plains region, a parallel system of settlement was developed, and formed a sort of "border" comprised of a combination of groups of hunters, gatherers, and farmers (Wachtel 2004). This true "human frontier" prevented the expansion of Andean groups into these territorial domains, and also held off Iberian colonial advances in the region for almost three centuries.

Over the course of little more than half a century (1691–1767), the Jesuits established themselves in the tierras bajas and founded mission complexes in which indigenous people of different origins and speakers of different languages gathered into reducciones. In these missions, the native peoples were subjected to the Christian faith and to compulsory work, although this does not mean that they became "acculturated" or adhered to European customs. The natives gave new and different meanings to everything that was offered to them and/or they were forced to accept into their lives. Indians and missionaries, in a constant flow of exchanges and interchanges, changed themselves and were modified by the missionary experience, which demonstrates that neither cultures nor ethnic identities are static and can be seen as essential.

The Expulsion of the Jesuits and the Situation of the Indians

In the year 1767, under the rule of Charles III (1759-1788), Spain put an end to reduction work with the expulsion of the Jesuits from South America. The interests of the State and the Church in this period were increasingly disparate. Among other things, it was said that usurpation of the sovereignty of the Crown in the reductions and incitement to rebellion arose from the Jesuits. Furthermore, there were complaints about the non-payment of tithes and disputes with other orders in relation to the Ignatians. After the expulsion of the Jesuits, the missions were transferred, especially Franciscan and secular priests, and later, the civil servants. Many of the Chiquitano people did not accept the new impositions, and even believed that the Jesuits would return.

It was then that the first non-indigenous inhabitants after the missionaries arrived from Santa Cruz de la Sierra to Chiquitania, where they founded ranches using the cattle from the reductions. Some of the natives, especially those who had not spent much time in the missions, went back into the wilds and tried to resume their old way of life; others remained and tried to maintain the order and customs that they had adopted in the reductions. The conflicts between the new priests and the employees, their inability to manage the reductions, the intensive exploitation of the indigenous people by religious and lay authorities, the recruitment of mission inhabitants for labor by the ranchers, and this group's resistance against the new order resulted in the gradual decay of the system, which was finally abolished in the 1850s.

After independence in 1825, the government of the new Republic of Bolivia divided the land in Chiquitania among non-Indians and the mestizos of Santa Cruz. Workforce needs were filled through government imposition of empadronamiento forzoso upon the Chiquitanos. In practical terms, this system meant enslaving the indigenous peoples, who became the property of their employers and could be sold along with the land. The reduction system was abolished by the government during the nineteenth century, and certainly considered the very liberal ideas which were in vogue at that time. Inspired by these ideas, the French traveler José Esteban Grondona wrote the Descripción Sinóptica de la Provincia de Chiquitos (Grondona 1942), which contained important information about the region and a scathing criticism of the reduction system which was still in force at that time.

Grondona blamed the backwardness of the province on three main causes: the personal contributions which many indigenous peoples were subjected to, known as tributos or impuestos; the slavery with which so many other Indians were subjugated; and the absence of the right to free trade, since the natives were under the tutelage of governors and administrators.

The traveler points out that the natives of Chiquitos were subject to:

> [...] a la pesadícima faena de un trabajo personal, por tres días por semana al servicio del Estado, que aún cuando no diese lugar a un sinnúmero de abusos por parte de la autoridad, y no fuese malísimamente distribuido [...], por su sola enormidad bastaria para ocasionar los más terribles efectos (Grondona 1942, [s. p.]).[4]

For the first half of the 19th century, the information the French naturalist Alcide d'Orbigny registered with regard to the Chiquitano people is equally valuable. D'Orbigny visited the former missions of Chiquitos and Mojos, appreciating the skills of the native peoples in playing classical music, skills which developed during the Jesuit period and are maintained to this day by the modern Chiquitano people in Bolivia. He noted, for example, that the Chiquitano women spun cotton, as they had done in the missions (apud Krekeler, p. 138). In visits made to the former Jesuit reductions, D'Orbigny found that the local languages of various groups had disappeared or were spoken by few people, "on a vu dans les missions, les idiomes de la disparaître minorité, remplacés par les dialectes des nations plus nombreuses" (D'Orbigny 1845, p. 172). [5] The Chiquitano language predominated at the expense of the Arawak and Chapacura languages which were still spoken at that time.

At this time, according to the American historian Cynthia Radding:

> The border between Chiquitos and Mato Grosso was porous and poorly defined – traversed by Indians and Creoles alike, seeking everyday supplies like iron implements, lantern oil, and even soap–yet it constituted the binational boundary between Bolivia and the Brazilian empire. From east to west, muleteers, cattle drivers, merchants, fugitive slaves, and others "of the miserable class" passed from Brazil to the department of Santa Cruz in the hopes of selling their wares or taking

[4] Translation: "[…] the exceedingly heavy personal labor, three days a week at the service of the State, that even if it was not followed by a countless number of abuses on the part of the authority, and if it were not distributed in an absolutely malicious manner [...], just by its enormity was sufficient to cause the most terrible effects."

[5] Translation: "I have seen in the missions, the languages of minorities disappear and are replaced by the dialects of the more numerous nations."

> refuge in the pueblos and estancias of Chiquitos (Radding 2005, p. 302-304; italics in the original).

Demographic data on the Chiquitanos for the first half of the nineteenth century are scarce. The 1805 and 1825 censuses respectively record 21,951 and 17,286 indigenous people living in the old reductions, which from that period came to be called pueblos. During the wars for Bolivian independence (1809–1825), the population of the pueblos became loyal to the Spanish Crown and the troops, which were mostly composed of indigenous Chiquitanos, were crushed in 1815 in the Battle of Santa Barbara. After the Battle of Ayacucho, which marked the surrender of the royal troops, annexation of the old Chiquitos Province in Brazil was proposed. And although Dom Pedro I had proclaimed the annexation of the province to the Brazilian empire on April 24, 1825 in the former Santa Ana Mission, the Luso-Brazilian emperor himself understood the act to be inadequate, and nullified the action of the local government, which did not spare the Empire energetic protests from the newly-created Bolivian government (Parejas Moreno; Suárez Salas 1992, p 153-154; Soares 2003; Costa 2008).

A census conducted in 1826 at the orders of Santa Cruz de la Sierra mayor Jose Miguel de Velasco recorded 17,315 indigenous people, which in a way confirms the data from the 1825 census. Four years later, in 1830, Alcide D'Orbigny recorded 15,316 indigenous people living in the same region (apud Tonelli Justiniano 2004, p. 170). The French naturalist attributed this decrease over such a short time to smallpox epidemics that ravaged Chiquitania, in addition to widespread food shortages. D'Orbigny was one of the first travelers to publicize the mineral wealth of the Chiquitania in his writings. He not only attested to the presence of gold, but also iron, copper, mica, silver, tin, and even precious stones.

The existence of gold in the region was reported in 1844, and soon spread throughout Chiquitania, which was invaded by non-indigenous people from Santa Cruz as well as foreigners. At this time the village of Santa Rosa de la Mina developed, which had previously been called Quebrada Ancha. "Gold fever" swept the region until the early 1890s, when income from the excavations began to decrease considerably. The indigenous people did not benefit economically from this activity, and did not even glimpse the possibility of exploiting the precious metals and stones, since they were only used as labor in the extraction activities in the service of non-indigenous people. Unfortunately, no demographic data were found for Chiquitania in the 1855 census.

In 1880, the Bolivian polymath Gabriel René Moreno referred to the "economic and social deterioration" in the region, which he observed as follows:

> Chiquitos, en los últimos cincuenta años [1830-1880], ha experimentado mudanzas muy grandes. Sus naturales han entrado en pleno periodo de decadencia, han perdido su fuerza engendradora y productora. [...] [os vícios introduzidos pelos não-indígenas] junto con los desarreglos administrativos de procedencia boliviana [...] [explicam] el estado de aniquilamiento presente (apud Tonelli Justiniano 2004, p. 192-193).[6]

The "estado de aniquilamiento" cited by Moreno refers to the suppression of the Jesuit reduction system. According to the author, instead of improving the conditions of the Chiquitano, the removal of this system deepened the economic decline of the region throughout the nineteenth century, placing the indigenous people into an oppressive working system, practically slavery. Although it was the Jesuits who introduced sugarcane into Chiquitania, it was in the nineteenth century that it large amounts of alcohol began to be manufactured in the region, which subjugated the indigenous people through addiction, converting them into bonded laborers of the chacras, the establecimientos, and the estancias. Additionally, rubber extraction in the late nineteenth century and the first two decades of the twentieth century in Bolivia and Brazil was a factor in the dramatic decrease in the population of the Chiquitanos (Lema Garret 2008).

Another important factor in the life of the Chiquitanos in the twentieth century was the construction of the Santa Cruz de la Sierra-Corumbá railway (ferrocarril) between 1938 and 1954. The tracks, which passed through Chiquitania, led to spatial rearrangement of the old villages and the old pueblos, causing the expulsion of part of the indigenous population to other localities, including Brazil (José Da Silva 2012). The Indians once again found themselves compelled to serve as labor, as in other times and situations. The 1953 agrarian reform meant changes in working relationships between indigenous and non-indigenous people; these were not felt immediately by the pueblos originários of the tierras bajas, which until the 1960s only received

[6] Translation: "Chiquitos, in the last fifty years [1830-1880], has experienced very great changes. Its population has come into a period of complete decadence, they have lost their productive force. [...] [the vices introduced by the non-indigenous people] along with the administrative disorders of Bolivian origin [...] [explain] the present state of annihilation."

lengths of fabric to make their own clothing as payment for their labor. For those who had already been sold along with the land and cattle as part of the property, the Chiquitanos saw other possibilities in the second half of the twentieth century.

CONCLUSION

Bolivia became an independent republic on August 6, 1825 and the leaders of the new country had to deal with a strong indigenous presence in the midst of a population (just under one million inhabitants) which was mostly illiterate and had been subjected to slavery until that time. The leaders of the country's first republican phase wanted to transform the social, economic, and political structure of the new nation by enacting laws that would lead to structural reforms. Notable among these reforms are the conversion of intendencies into departments, attempts to eliminate the "indigenous contribution," and promotion of agrarian reform, usurping the ownership of lands from the pueblos originarios and delivering them to non-native people.

Throughout the nineteenth century, indigenous labor was exploited in countless ways in the newly-created Bolivian Republic. The exploitation of rubber (goma) in the second half of the 19th century consumed the lives of thousands of indigenous people and represented another chapter in this population's history of servitude, which began even before the arrival of the Europeans with the Inca Empire. The Jesuit period (1691-1767) meant a reordering of the relations between the pueblos originários and their environment. The expulsion of the missionaries and the abandonment of the old missions (reducciones) profoundly impacted the people who inhabited the tierras bajas, notably the Chiquitanos.

The Chiquitanos, who are one of the largest ethnic groups in the Bolivian ethnic panorama, participated in the Chaco War (1932-1935) and lived under a labor regime analogous to slavery in the nineteenth century and most of the twentieth century. The Bolivian Republic, divided into a non-indigenous political and intellectual elite and an indigenous population which was the majority but which had been kept out of power, had immense difficulties in dealing with the massive presence of Indians, both in the altiplano and in the plains (tierras bajas). Centuries of exploitation of the different ethnic groups, first by the Spanish and then by their descendants, created a country that was very rich for a select few.

Only at the beginning of the twenty-first century would Bolivia finally be recognized as a multi-ethnic state with the election of a president of indigenous origin, the Aymara Evo Morales. Profound changes are underway, not only within the framework of the laws, but above all in daily life and in society. However, the challenges posed by centuries of denying the majority presence of the pueblos originários put the country into a situation of looking back to its own past (pre-colonial and colonial) and looking forward to a future that will be quite distinct from the one planned in the first half of the nineteenth century by the "founders" of the Republic. The Chiquitano people and other indigenous peoples of Chiquitania face new and different challenges.

References

Birk, G. (2000). "Forest owners: management of natural resources by Chiquitano Indians of Bolivia". Santa Cruz de la Sierra: APCOB.

Carvalho, R. (2005). "Manual History of Bolivia a view from the plain". Santa Cruz de la Sierra: Mavarú.

Costa, J. E. F. M. da. (2008). "The formation of the Chiquitano territory". In: Silva, J. A. F. (Ed.) *Studies on the Chiquitanos in Brazil and Bolivia: history, language, culture and territoriality* (pp. 167-221). Goiânia: UCG.

D'orbigny, A. D. (1845). Fragment of a journey to the center of America Meridionale. Paris/Strasbourg: Bertrand/Levrault.

Grondin, M. (1984). "The peasant revolution in Bolivia". Sao Paulo: Brasiliense.

Grondona, J. E. (1942). "Synoptic description of the province of Chiquitos". Sucre: San Francisco Javier University.

Hany, W. S. (2007). "The high Peru the Republic of Bolivia: the formation of the Bolivian state". In: Navarro, E. M. M. et al. (Eds.). *40 years of the Pantanal Campus - UFMS: contributions for the regional development* (pp. 325-346). Campo Grande: UFMS.

Hollweg, M. G. (1977). *The racial myth and Bolivian man*. Santa Cruz de la Sierra: Orphans.

Klein, H. S. (1991). *Pre-Incan independence period*. Sao Paulo: Brasiliense.

Klein, H. S. (1994). *History of Bolivia*. La Paz: Youth.

Krekeler, B. (1995). *Chiquitanos history*. Santa Cruz de la Sierra: APCOB.

José da Silva, G. (2012). *Changing identities: The Kamba in the Brazil-Bolivia*. Goiânia: UFG.

Lema Garret, A. M. (2008). *The meaning of silence: chiquitana hand work in the Bolivian East in the early twentieth century.* La Paz: U-PIEB (University for Strategic Research in Bolivia).

Mesa, J. de, Gisbert, T., & Mesa Gisbert, C. D. (2007). *History of Bolivia. La Paz, Bolivia*: Gisbert y Cia.

Montaño Aragón, M. (1977). *Bolivian cultural anthropology.* La Paz: Municipal House of Culture Franz Tamayo.

United Nations. (2005) *Cepal. Indigenous Peoples of Bolivia: Sociodemographic diagnosis from the 2001 census.* Santiago: ONU.

Parejas Moreno, A.; Suárez Salas, V. (1992). *Chiquitos: story of a utopia. Santa Cruz de la Sierra*: CORDECRUZ/Private University of Santa Cruz de la Sierra.

Radding, C. (2005). *Landscapes of power and identity: comparative histories in the Sonoran Desert and the forests of Amazonia from Colony to Republic.* Durham/London: Duke University Press.

Richard, N. (Ed.). (2008). *Bad war: Indians in the Chaco War (1932-1935).* Assumption/Paris: Servilibro/Museo del Barro/CoLibris.

Riester, J. (2005). *Iyambae - Be Free: the Chaco War (1932-1935) - Bilingual Guarani - Castilian texts.* Santa Cruz de la Sierra: APCOB.

Rivera Cusicanqui, S. (2008). "Colonialism and ethnic resistance in Bolivia: a view from the coca markets". In: ROSEN, F. (Ed.). *Empire and dissent: The United States and Latin America.* Durham: Duke University Press.

Rocha, L. M. (2006). "The configuration of the multi-ethnic and multi-cultural State in Bolivia". In: ROCHA, L. M. (Ed.). *Ethnicity and nation.* (pp. 09-20). Goiânia: Cânone.

Silva, S. A. da. (1997). *Tailoring dreams: the story of a group of Bolivian immigrants in São Paulo.* São Paulo: Paulinas.

Soares, M. do S. C. (2003). *The provisional government of Mato Grosso and the issue of annexation of Chiquitos Province to the Brazilian Empire (1821-1825).* Cuiabá: UFMT.

Stearman, A. M. (1987). *Camba and Colla: migration and development in Santa Cruz, Bolivia.* La Paz: Juventud (Youth).

Tonelli Justiniano, O. (2004). *Historical, social and economical review Chiquitania. Santa Cruz de la Sierra*: El País.

Wachtel, N. (2004). "The Indians and the Spanish conquest". In: Bethell, L. (Ed.). *History of Latin America: Latin America Colonial.* São Paulo/Brasilia: Edusp/Alexandre de Gusmão Foundation.

In: Bolivia
Editor: Glen Mendoza
ISBN: 978-1-63484-886-2

Chapter 2

EASTERN BORDERS OF BOLIVIA: EARLY DECADES OF THE 19TH CENTURY

Ernesto Cerveira de Sena *
Federal University of Mato Grosso (UFMT), Brazil

ABSTRACT

This essay deals with the construction of Bolivia's eastern border, shortly after independence, before the Empire of Brazil. Becoming an independent country in 1825, not only from Spain but also from the territorial claims of Lima and Buenos Aires, Bolivia only made its first treaty limits with Brazil in 1867, after several setbacks. Regardless, only diplomats nominated by their central governments did not do a treaty like this. Before that, the local population, such as indigenous groups, settlers from both sides, black slaves as well as local governments have developed strategies to intend face the border area, with different interests and influence in that. To government administrators, the important thing was to ensure the "ownership" of the given territory, to others, as settlers and African slaves, the frontier meant to change social conditions possibilities.

Keywords: Bolivia, nation building, eastern boundaries, local rulers

---

* Corresponding author: Professor and researcher from Universidade Federal de Mato Grosso (UFMT), Brazil. Doctorate from Universidade de Brasília (UnB).CNPq/BR supported. E-mail: ernesto.sena@gmail.com.

What today constitutes the "Bolivian East" began to be occupied by the Spanish in the early sixteenth century, and since then has taken on a character of "frontier," that is, a land on the margin of the economic and social systems. While it was a projection of new areas to be colonized by Spaniards and Mestizos, it was also one whose security region was considered vulnerable, possible just to disappear under indigenous groups attacks, or even be absorbed by another empire, the Portuguese, advancing from the direction of the rising sun.

With the news of the discovery of gold, silver and other precious minerals, many Spanish and other European organized vessels to cross the Atlantic with the intention of exploring the new continent. Among these expeditions, there was commanded by Juan de Solís (1512) who found the 'big sweet sea." They thought it was part of the ocean because of the width and length of the river. Undone such a mistake, soon came to be baptized the River Plate, and never change again, while none finding any silver in it. The Spanish given such name because of the hope of being a path that would lead to vast treasures not yet known on Earth.

With the Solís travel, it spread the news that there would be a land in the interior of the continent with an unimaginable abundance of precious metals. It began to develop the myth of El Dorado, the Paititi or Mojos, names related to alleged places of which it was thought, in addition to containing a silver mountain, also have plenty of food, milk sources and honey gushing all part. This news motivated further to several European to venture on ships that were heading to America, fleeing poverty in their continent. At the same time, on the Pacific coast, Pizarro had hit the Peru, whose conquest would end in 1541 (García Recio, 1988)

Given the situation, the Spanish Crown divided the territory envisioned south of Peru, in three jurisdictions outside the Lima area: one which would be Tucumán, in the current Argentina, another in what would be Chile, and the third in what has become Asuncion of Paraguay (Malamud, 2005). To occupy these parties had sent several convoys of ships to the River Plate. Some succeeded in founding settlements but were soon destroyed by the Indians. Buenos Aires, for example, created in 1536, but soon its small population was decimated, after being re-founded only in 1580. Among these expeditions made by boat, one founded the city of Asuncion, in 1537, in a large tributary of the River Plate, the Paraguay River, in a strategic place to build a village with a port for boats, and thus form a basis for expeditions, or "*entradas*" as Spaniards spoke.

The success of the Assumption's formation was due in large part to the adaptation of the Spanish with the Guarani people and the place where since early mixed biologically and culturally, although there were, once a while, conflicts between various social groups. In any case, it was from Assumption that left an expedition that eventually form the first city of Santa Cruz, in 1561, where is now San José de Chiquitos. Its founder, Ñuflo de Chaves, made two trips to Lima, residence of the Viceroy of Peru, to create an autonomous governing body. To get the idea of enrichment mind by achievements and discoveries, Ñuflo de Chaves believed with certainty that there could found astonishing discoveries in a place called Mojos by indigenous initially (Recio, p. 45). Then, the new governing body were named Mojos Y Santa Cruz, and the city of Santa Cruz was its capital. At the same time they founded several other towns in the region, such as Santo Domingo de Nueva Rioja (1557), La Barranca (1559) and Santiago del Puerto (1592), but all they disappeared due to the lack of food and Indians attack (García Recio, p. 21).

Much of the success of Ñuflo de Chaves to establish a settlement was due to his long experience of two decades of relationship with indigenous groups in Paraguay. To found Santa Cruz had dealings with the Indians Chiriguanos, that later they would kill him, when new government rules broken his covenant (Martinez, 2013).

Before long, Santa Cruz would be transplanted to another place, known as "Cotoca" between the years 1601 and 1604, because of Indian attacks and little chance of survival of their small population. For the same time had been founded the town of San Lorenzo de La la Frontera, west of Santa Cruz. With continued hunger, poor harvests, finally, in 1622, Santa Cruz fused with San Lorenzo de la Frontera, on the right bank of the River Pyraí. The official name of the place was Santa Cruz de la Sierra, and the San Lorenzo was the saint patron of the new location. Santa Cruz then became known as the "wanderer city," but the third in which it was where it is today (Penã et al. 2011).

In all these years of "conquest" of space, Santa Cruz suffered from the lack of settlers. Often expeditions were organized towards Mojos, where they hoped to find the riches of which we speak, many of which annihilated by people who defended their land. Others just could not find anything of value to compensate. Since the sixteenth century, many expeditions contained clerics to try to conquer the indigenous souls, including seeking to establish religious missions. But much failed from the start due to the open hostility of the indigenous groups who tried to reject the penetration in their areas (Coello de la Rosa, 2013).

On the other hand, also, expeditions sought to capture Indians to be practically slave labor force on the plantations and urban services, despite the Spanish Crown and the Church ban the enslave them. Regardless, it ended up forming a society characterized by miscegenation, the most extreme point of the Spanish border in a region considered quite isolated compared to other human groups who obeyed the Spanish jurisdictions.

Thus, the situation of the limit region occurred since the beginning. Here it is understood as a "border" to stay on the edge of the Spanish claim to spatial occupations. It's border also for being the place where had contacted Spanish cultural model with indigenous cultural in their territory. We also add that it was the border, as it was an ahead of where they expected to build a base to move to other places, bringing the Spanish model to new areas, fighting to achievement in both lands, as people. It was also a "frontier space" whose boundaries were open, although the rulers of the Iberian Peninsula seek to trace its limits abstractly and jurisdictions appointments drawing maps, encompassing and separating land and people who barely knew them or else completely unaware humans and places.

Thus, Paula Peña points out that when Santa Cruz was installed on the edge of Rio Guapay, it left the Asuncion's area of influence, and started to be a part of Audience of Charcas jurisdiction. Charcas would later be the basis for the formation of post-independent Bolivian soil. Besides, Santa Cruz acquired a characteristic of almost total isolation from other Spanish populations. Then, it developed its propers characteristics, without the production of precious metals such as the Andean region, based on agricultural production, making wars and alliances with indigenous, miscegenation, but being, above all, a starting point for new expeditions who wanted to find riches in Mojos. The isolation aspect provided considerable autonomy, which facilitated enslave warlike indigenous groups. Thus, Santa Cruz ended up taking the title of "city" but also being named a "province" (Peña hasburn, 2011, 20-26).

However, if Santa Cruz de la Sierra had a great degree of independence from other Spanish colonies, the existence of this city was of interest to the viceroy of Peru, the maximum governing body of the region, as well as Charcas audience. It would be the most advanced core, an "inner boundary" against the advance of Chiriguanos Indians and other indigenous groups, being an obstacle to the progress of the Portuguese pioneers belonging to an enemy colonial power, threatening to reach the very rich silver mines that existed in the Andes.

Commercially, your little trade was made to meet the demands of the mines of Potosi, the hard way, while it became virtually closed its connection to Assunción of Paraguay, they had similar products. The only product that Santa Cruz could export in a compensatory way was sugar, whose activity had some success even in the seventeenth century (García Récio, 1989, 33-36).

The situation in the region changes significantly with the installation of religious missions of Chiquitos and Mojos. The first mission was installed in the region called the Mojos in 1682 by the Jesuits. Soon the Jesuits also founded the missions in place that would be Chiquitos, in 1691, the region closer to Santa Cruz than that of Mojos (Peña Hasburn, 2011, 23).

The missions had various roles in this frontier region because Cruceños/ Spaniards could not install settlements in Chiquitos region. It was mainly due to the strong territorial defense of several indigenous groups, which often, could establish alliances among themselves against the invading element. Against weapons of the Spaniards, used since moats with traps, through the construction of observation towers, to poisoned arrows (Moreira da Costa, 2008).

Another factor critical was the lack of enough people in Santa Cruz de la Sierra to build a village in a hostile environment for new settlers. Therefore, the missions could resist several assaults of its contenders. The Jesuits appeared as an economical way, valid culturally because they spread the "Christian civilization," and, politically, could occupy the lands threatened by the Portuguese, who had also been behind wealth. At the same time also prevented the Portuguese pioneers of one hand and Cruceños/Spaniards on the other to caught Indians to turn them into slaves.

To the Jesuits undertake the construction missions were important because it had no major parishes in key areas of Spanish America, occupied by other orders that had first arrived in Peru and Mexico. Thus, even before the missions, the Jesuits accompanied the Cruzeños in the expeditions. If they discovered the famous "El Dorado," or something like that, if they built cities and administrative bodies, they would get the bishoprics, and even riches, because the criterion of "conquest" which established the key positions for that first arrived in new areas. With the missions, surely the work was much more arduous. However, the conquest of new souls would be the rewarding side of many products, in a particular production model, what soon would implement in the borderlands (Coello de la Costa, 2013, 91).

The work to establish the missions was in some way benefited when indigenous groups in Chiquitanía went to Santa Cruz de la Sierra request alliance with the Cruzeños to face the Chiriguanos groups, others indigenous groups and the Portugueses who took them captive. Therefore, the missions went on Chiquitos suffering various human and material losses but managed to organize settlements. They served effectively to fight against hostile groups to missioned Indians, now Christianized, while also braked the rush of Portuguese. Thus, the missions served as a wall protecting the Spanish area of the advances of Portugal, who also protected the real wealth in the Potosi in the Andes, and all Andean region.

In any case, the Portuguese occupied what is now Mato Grosso, the present neighbor of the department of Santa Cruz. The occupation was mainly due to the discovery of gold and diamonds, and the promise that there would be many other sources of minerals in that hinterland of South America. At the same time, it appeared that the rivers of the Plata (Silver) basin would reach even those central areas of the subcontinent. Especially the Paraguay River, one of its rivers, would link up to the Amazon basin, forming supposedly the "Island-Brazil," which becoming a myth, based on the legendary accounts of travelers and rulers of the seventeenth century, used by Brazil Empire diplomats in the nineteenth century (Magnoli, 1997).

In the context of several Spanish reforms of the eighteenth century, known generically as "Bourbon's Reforms," the missions were extinguished, and the Jesuits expelled from America. The Spanish crown appropriated their land and property. The changes were based on an idea to rationalize the colonial productions, so it should send more dividends to Spain. The missions, before, had become successful in their productions of various articles, from sugar to musical instruments. With the extinction of the company of Jesus, the missions who performed very independent, the Jesuit's area would be Spanish territory, that is, people and things would be linked to the monarchy, under its rules. The frontier area of Jesuits was not more an element that has "weird" in the face of new ideas of the great Spanish Empire, which needed to be more close to its areas. It is its necessity to face of competitive colonial powers and to "survive" in the middle of wars Europe itself.

It was precise to be better utilized the resources of the marginal areas of the imperial system, which was created the Viceroyalty of the Silver in 1776, directly linking the port of Buenos Aires to Spain. At the same time, Spain sought to strengthen this area, making Audience of Charcas part of the new viceroy, who, as we have already noted, had the fabulous mines of Potosi, and now included Santa Cruz with their governorates of Chiquitos and Mojos. This measure has caused protests from Lima, formerly route from the goods produced and received in Potosí, and it possessed its jurisdiction as far as the undefined border with the Portuguese America.

When erupted the wars of independence, there were not only struggles of Latin Americans against the Spaniards. There were also conflicts between different regions than was the Spanish Empire in America. It was precisely the rivalry between Limeños and Porteños (these, who were living in Buenos Aires), which gave rise to Bolivia. Lima claimed the jurisdictions of the old Viceroyalty of Peru, as it existed before the reform of 1776. For its part, Buenos Aires wanted to have not only what is now Argentina, but also what today is Uruguay, Paraguay, and Bolivia. Both sides failed the Charcas annexation attempts, given the attitude of General Sucre, the right arm of Simon Bolivar, to make a new country, uncoupled the two ancient viceroyalties (Roca, 2007).

THE NEW COUNTRY AND THE BORDER

Due the independences, many countries were forging from of the old Spanish Empire. A general feature introduced liberal institutions, such as Congress, Judicial, and Executive, free press, some bureaucracy which calculates and applies population policies, discourses on education, and the foundation of cultural and scientific associations, that establish pathways to progress targets. However, another factor that marked the new countries would provide what is "our" territory, as far as it goes, as far as the "neighbor" country can reach.

Territorial issues would not be established from one day to the other. The governors and state representatives needed before many diplomatic conversations as they searched for to survey the potential for the production of wealth and evaluated their geopolitical importance of the border. In any case, the construction of boundaries for every new National States was a contingency to be solved, since the territory was one of the strongest symbols of new political instances in the 19th (Foucher, 1986).

The first treaty between Bolivia and Brazil was signed in 1867. The area treated, the Bolivian East, was the one that least attention received from the Bolivian government. Bolivia, to try to recover from independence war, invested much where it knew had some export product, as in Potosi, but without being able not nearly what it had been at the time of the colony. There were also investments for the construction of railways, as it required at that time, but until then, the area of Santa Cruz was not included with these and other forms of investments.

Communications like a railway track, a steamboat, passable roads, were clearly seen as a factor to achieve the dream "civilization" and make strides toward "progress" as was said at the time. However, most of the Bolivian population was indigenous and mestizos, which put in the discussion on how to build a "civilized" country with so many people perceived to be refractory to the "symbols" of progress, such as were the communications media and ways of behaving and being similar to the European.

Regardless, in the 1840s, the period of Ballivián president (1841-1847), investments were designed in the eastern region, hitherto little worthy of attention. Sought to establish again religious missions in the eastern areas of Bolivia, so that the missioners could civilize the Indians and become them productive to the market by way of Christianization of the indigenous groups of the border (García Jordan, 2003). However, ended up being more successful missions who worked with indigenous groups in "Amazon frontier" than in Platinum region. On the other hand, was Brazil's empire who provided for the establishment of missions in its west, mainly aiming to ownership and control of the rivers that ran to the south, as the river Paraguay, that is, in the region where it would make the limits with Paraguay and Bolivia.

There were disagreements over where were the boundaries between countries. In general, Bolivia complained that its limits would be as it had been in the Treaty of Portugal and Spain, the Santo Ildefonso agreement, made in 1777. Brazil went on to claim the principle of Uti Possidetis, after hesitation about what policy to adopt: each country having continued his possessions. Now it was clear that the Empire had advanced over land that could have been in Spain during the colonial era. On the other hand, the government of the Empire of Brazil argued that it could not use a treaty Colony Era as defining the limits. Because in addition to having occurred others treaties after 1777, before independences there was a war between Spain and Portugal in the early Nineteenth Century, which cancel any previous agreement.

As we signed, the agreement on limits was made only in 1867. Before this agreement, it is necessary to show some strategies of various actors. Already during the wars of independence, local governments of Mato Grosso province sought to attract Indians from ancient Chiquitos Missions to pass to the territory once thought to be Brazilian. In the absence of settlers, the Chiquitanos occupy a particular area that interested the Brazil Empire. So, they could soon also become "national" of the province, helping to strengthen the "Brazilian" presence in border areas. Added to this, unlike other Indians, how then were the Bororos, the Chiquitanos had the practice of agriculture and knew other abilities such as carpentry and raise plantation. Finally, we note that the Chiquitanos could also defalcate the same population group (governors estimated the number of people also because of wars) of the neighboring country, who sooner or later would map the limits.

For Chiquitanos, migrate to Brazil means the expectation of better conditions. In this way, they traded with the Brazilians to move aside. In fact, this happened since colonial times when Indians of the border area were negotiating if they or not changed the place of residence (LENY, Caselli). That was how, for example, Vila Maria, today Cáceres, was implemented on the banks of the Paraguay River, in the late eighteenth century (Volpato, 1987). It was made mainly by indigenous people from Spanish Empire. If this trade was useful for indigenous groups, so was for the Portuguese Empire for scoring occupying part of the territory that mattered.

Cross the border during the colonial period to the black slaves could also mean better conditions and even the "freedom." The National Period (after independence), Bolivia did advertisement that was "free land of slavery." This "free land" was predicted even in its first Constitution. However, in other legal provisions was delayed abolition. In the Constitutions of 1853 and 1868, it repeated that anyone who was born or entered in Bolivia would be considered "free." However, in practice, the black slavery continued, for example, a slave owner who lent "their" black to work in the church in Santa Cruz jurisdiction (Sena, 2013). In practice, the black slavery continued, for example, a slave owner who lent "their" black to work in the church. However, the work of black slaves of hand was far from being the dominant as it was in Brazil. In Bolivia, most were Indians, while across the limits, in Mato Grosso, the slaves were most of the workforce besides free and poor blacks (Volpato, 1993).

Since when the news came that the troops commanded by Bolivar (actually, it was not him, but the groups commanded by Marshal Sucre) was about to take Santa Cruz de la Sierra, spread a rumor that he would invade Mato Grosso and free the slaves (Seckinger, 1985). Most probably it had been news of black battalions who fought for independence in Venezuela and River Plate, where blacks earned the freedom to fight against the Spanish, which may have nourished the hope of the captives be set free by "The Liberator" as it was known Bolívar. However, it made no such invasion, there was even less freedom for the slaves immediately in Bolivia, as many expected, and how Bolivia made its merchandising.

Regardless, the blacks were constant breakouts from the colonial period. With the wars of independence and the idea of "freedom," it was thought that those who cross the border would get manumission because of the newly created country propaganda. Thus, slave masters, governors, and militaries have taken barriers to try to contain the various escapes that occurred. Thus, they had military posts in the ways they discovered leaks. Also, offer pay "ransom" for Bolivians to return the slaves. Brazilians had even led an expedition of soldiers with its commander taking money and weapons, to bring slaves who were in Bolivia when he returned.

At one point in the 1840s, the Mato Grosso authorities began to complain that the Bolivians were no longer being returned slaves as before. The president of the Mato Grosso province sent letters claiming the "property rights" of Brazilians. Nothing worked. In fact, Bolivia had the trump card in negotiations with Brazil could just negotiate an extradition treaty with the Treaty limits. We note that, usually, when two countries signed an agreement about territories between countries, usually there were other points together, as trade between the both, rivers that could navigate, conditions and requirements (often reciprocal) to enter and exit the neighboring territory. Regardless, it was a series of intentions that linked to the signing of the treaty limits.

Thus, the Empire of Brazil sought to occupy certain spaces in the border area also with settlers, ceding lands to them. Unfortunately, for the rulers, among the population considered small, there were not enough people willing to move to these areas, for those who lived away from the capital often suffered from Indian attacks, such as the Bororo, among other difficulties in settling at many miles away from the capital, Cuiabá.

Finally, in addition to several actors who made their strategies at the border, taking into account the new National States, it is important to observe the settings of international relations in this region of the South American subcontinent. The first treaty was made during the war of Brazil against Paraguay with the Brazilian Empire having allies Argentina and Uruguay. One of the main reasons for the war was precisely the territorial boundary between the countries in the region formation and navigation in the La Plata basin, which were the port of Buenos Aires and were of Montevideo. It was for these waterways that reached the interior of Argentina, Uruguay, in addition to interest the Empire to stability your navigation to Mato Grosso, on the border with Bolivia. In fact, the Empire had been the big Buenos Aires rival in the quest for Silver hegemony area even before starting the independence processes. Particular policy setting enabled the peace and alliance between Buenos Aires and Rio de Janeiro, which, before the Paraguayan initial invasion, that in a political miscalculation, it was without the support of the interior of Argentina (Buenos Aires opponents) and Blancos (Uruguayan group that previously had tied to the Assumption). Still, the Paraguayans fought a war against the powers of the region, taking five years to be fully defeated, whose effects of the conflict were extremely harmful to the republic Guarani.

Bolivia initially drew support for Paraguay. However, the Empire presented a proposal which turned out to be of interest to Bolivia, removing the conflict in Silver (Doratioto, 2002). If Brazil occupies certain areas of the border zone, Bolivia could navigate freely through the Amazonian rivers. There was also the promise to build a road rail that would link Bolivia's eastern Amazon region by making available ports of the Atlantic. On the other hand, issues such as the deportation of slaves were left out, because it was the empire's Achilles heel when dealing with any diplomatic issue. A treaty, then, meant not belligerence between the parties. At the same time, an agreement would facilitate the "construction" of theirs territorial, even if it were not as they imagined.

CONCLUSION

A border treaty was not only done by diplomats. Before them, various social actors played their roles seeking to be subject to their fate, as slaves, Indians and even settlers and deserters who fled to the "other side." At the same time, local governments sought to correspond with general policies of his country, but also developed their own plans considering the local people.

The local rulers of eastern Bolivia, as their mayors of the Santa Cruz de La Sierra department who realized the impossibility of finding a way out by Plata (Silver River). While nearly saw the failure of various colonization attempts to establish a port to transport their goods and persons receiving and export goods. Thus, an exit through Amazon showed itself rewarding. She showed even more viable with the record of various wars and disputes in the platinum region. Throw the Silver, it was clear that Bolivia would not only be allowed Brazil to reach the sea for its east. Also, need agreements with Paraguay, Uruguay, and Buenos Aires, whose political instabilities were difficult to predict when to cease. The Amazon, only depend on good relations with a single country.

The rulers also sought to form a "memory" of the border, looking for documentations to "prove" the existence of "proto-nationals" or "national" in certain areas, to justify the idea of "Uti possidetis," even been quite sparse alleged the locations occupants in the border area. Bolivia, for its part, feeling more than Mato Grosso the lack of people in the area that should be settled. However, given the fragility of Bolivia in the decades after its inception, she sought some advantage with the slaves of Brazil in their quest for "freedom," regardless of the fact to your destination.

In any case, what just stressed in the agreement of 1867 was the possibility of navigating the Amazon and a railway. Bolivia was expecting to find a product that could motivate the migration of people to the border area, officially defined by the National States, even with the tiny possibility of control various people movement and way of life, such as indigenous peoples, who had another territorial conception. However, this is for another time.

REFERENCES

Coello de la Rosa, Alexandre (2013). "The missional activity of the Jesuits in the governorship of Santa Cruz de la Sierra (1587-1599)" *In Santa Cruz de la vieja, edited by* Isabelle Combés and Paula Peña Hasburn, 83-108. Santa Cruz de la Sierra: Gobierno Municipal autónomo de Santa Cruz de la Sierra.

Doratioto, Francisco (2002). *Damn war: new history of the Paraguayan War.* São Paulo: Cia. das Letras.

Foucher, Michel (1986). *The invention border.* Paris: F.E.D.N.

García Jordán, Pilar (2001). *Cruz and Arado, Rifles and speeches - Construction of the Easts in Peru and Bolivia 1820-1940.* Publisher IFEA/IEP: Lima.

García Recio (1988). José María. *Analysis of a frontier society. Santa Cruz de la Sierra in the sixteenth and seventeenth centuries.* Sevilla: South Charts/Provincial de Sevilla/National Historical Archive of Bolivia.

Magnoli, Demétrio (1997). *The Home Body - geographical imagination and foreign policy in Brazil (1808-1912).* São Paulo: Ed. Unesp/Moderna.

Martinez, Cecília (2013). "Of Paraguay to the Piedemonte, friends adversaries: Ñuflo Chavez and Guarani em the conquest of Santa Cruz de la Sierra." In *Santa Cruz de la vieja*, edited by Isabelle Combés and Paula Peña Hasburn, p. 33-66. Santa Cruz de la Sierra: Autonomous Municipal Government of Santa Cruz de la Sierra, 2013.

Peña Hasbún, Paula, et al. (2011). *The ongoing construction of the Santa Cruz - a study on identity in Santa Cruz de la Sierra.* La Paz: Foundation PIEB, 2011.

Roca, José Luis (2007). *Neither with nor Lima Buenos Aires: The formation of a national state in Charcas*. La Paz, IFEA/Plural editors.

Sekinger, Ron L. (1985). "The issue of young children: a brief crisis in the Bolivian-Brazilian relations." *Journal of the University Gabriel René Moreno. Santa Cruz de la Sierra, 40*, 7-22.

Sena, Ernesto Cerveira de. (2013). "Leakage and re-enslavement in the border region. - Bolivia and Brazil in the first decades of national states." *Ibero-American Studies,* Porto Alegre, v. 39, n. 1, p. 82-98.

Volpato, Luiza Rios Ricci (1993). *Captives of the Hinterland.* São Paulo: Marco Zero. _____. (1987). *The land of conquest in poverty universe: the formation of the western border of Brazil 1719-1819.* São Paulo: HUCITEC.

In: Bolivia
Editor: Glen Mendoza

ISBN: 978-1-63484-886-2

Chapter 3

RESOURCE NATIONALISM AND ENVIRONMENTAL CHANGES*

Nidia Catherine González *
University of Bologna, Italy/Santo Tomás University, Colombia

ABSTRACT

Bolivia is the first Plurinational State in the world, in which the State, constitutionally, assures the coexistence of different nations in a common area. The creation of this new Bolivian State addresses processes of mass mobilisation which structure the history of this country, and which after the neoliberal reforms of the end of the eighties and in the nineties, reached the tipping point of questioning the traditional policies. The election of the first indigenous president in 2005 replied to said process of questioning and set different challenges for this national society and at the same time for the global society. From this perspective the objective of this article is to reflect on the complexity of the tensions among which emerged from resource nationalism, decentralisation, as well as communitarian politics related to the Bolivian case. This work is

* This article belongs to the research project entitled: "Governability in Latin America: plurinational constitutions and "resource nationalism" in the XXI century", which is financed by an interinstitutional cooperation agreement between the Political and Social Sciences Department of the University of Bologna (Italy) and the Institute of Socio-Historical Studies Fray Alonso de Zamora of the University Santo Tomás (Colombia).

* Nidia Catherine González, PhD in Philosophy and Political Science, Johannes Gutenberg University – Mainz (Germany). Currently is Research Associate of the Political and Social - Sciences Department of the University of Bologna.

structured in three parts. The first introductory part, presents the dynamic creation of the Plurinational State of Bolivia. The central part of the text is the second one, which analyses various elements: 1) the country's resource nationalism studied from the Latin-American and world context, characterising the tensions surrounding the institutionalisation of social movements and their grassroots struggles; 2) the regulation of the multilateral administration of the natural resources and the economic distribution of its profits, specifically in the case of the non-renewable, which were strategic in the preceding ten years; 3) the impacts of the resource prosperity on the state commitments of advancing in the construction of the new constitutional order refounded in 2009; and 4) the simultaneous challenges of the government Bolivian in the redistribution of wealth, poverty and inequality reduction, similarly in the advances in the climate change agenda. To close this second part, cases of decentralisation and of TIPNIS Park are briefly presented as examples of structural divisions between the State and the sectors of Bolivian society which tension is observed such as resolving the transition of extractivism on a large scale towards innovative means of sustainability. Finally, the last part of this chapter describes an environmental perspective which shows a contrast between capitalist production and the *Buen vivir* (well-being) models developed by the local Bolivian community, a fundamental contrast to understand the future of the Latin-American region. This contrast shows the fractures in the current urban capitalist modus vivendi and illustrates some communitarian practices, as alternative options to the global crisis.

Keywords: resource nationalism, environmental sustainability, plurinational state

INTRODUCTION: THE CONSTRUCTION OF THE PLURINATIONAL BOLIVIAN STATE

In recent years the influence of grassroots struggles and multiple processes of mobilisation in Bolivia have transformed its institutional political system, in which the Bolivian society has proposed to the world new models of institutional, social, ecological and political transformation (García Linera 2005; 2010: 9-43). Currently, the Plurinational Bolivian State accommodates the largest percentage of indigenous population on the American continent and thus, 90% of its inhabitants consider themselves indigenous (Pati, 2009: 34)[1]. Scenarios of mass social mobilisation such as the Water War, the Gas War, the constituent assembly Marches, for popular sovereignty, Territory and Natural Resources, and finally, the Coca Leaf Defence, were processes which expressed a maximum point of social and political tension with the traditional institutions on the part of the indigenous movements, the working class, the trade unions, and other popular sectors (Chávez/Mokrani, 2007; Rivera 2003; Yrigoren, 2010). At the same time this mobilisation's wave reaffirmed that the popular demands of the 1952 revolution, continued seeking other ways of organising the society. The case of the 1952 National Revolution in Bolivia is particular in Latin-American history, being considered by some historians as the first and only national working and agricultural revolution of the entire Continent (Mires, 1988: 158-278). During this uprising, agrarian reform was achieved the farm was removed as an economic, social and political structure. This revolution along with the Cuban revolution, has had the greatest national impact in the whole region and was organised by poor city dwellers, peasants, the unionised workers and the National Revolutionary Movement – NRM - against the State and in reply to the gradual process of land expropriation by the oligarchic minority (Mires, 1988; Cuscicanqui, 1984; Espasandín & Iglesias, 2007). Thus, in 1880, 50% of the land was in indigenous hands. In the period between the reform of President Melgarejo (1886) until 1930, the indigenous maintained the property of only less than a third. This, besides the Chaco War and the sale of territories to Brazil and Chile at the beginning of the XX century, all these circumstances evidenced the urgency to resolve a matter concern: "It was a nationwithout State and an State without nation" (Mires, 1998: 168).

At that historical moment the NRM was formed following principles: to fight for the nationalisation of mines and railways, to advocate for agrarian reform, to aim for industrial diversification and the creation of new sources of wealth through State's actions (Mires, 1988: 168; Klein, 1969). The 1952 revolution had rapid effects in favour of the mobilised sectors, as two thirds of the mining industry were nationalised; nevertheless these effects were minimized by the incursion of the Liberal party into the government, which came into power favoured by the influence of the United States of America. In Bolivia, the so called "tin men" inalliancewith the liberals and the churchrepressed indigenous and peasants (Mires, 1988; Klein, 1969). This

[1] According to the 2001 census, indigenous and original inhabitants represent 62% of the population, in contrast, social organisations recognise the presence of 90% among these ethnic groups (Pati, 2009:34).

same wave against revolutionary reform processes came to pass in reply to the Argentinian Peronism, the copper's nationalisation in Chile, besides, the Getulio Vargas reforms in Brazil (Zanatta, 2012). In this context during the distinct processes of nationalisation in Latin-America the North American politics influenced the definition of the ideological frontiers of the Cold War.

Under comparative analysis, the 1952 revolution in regard to that undertaken by the Bolivian people between 2000 and 2005, can be seen that both processes of mobilisation had the aim of political re-founding of the State, in terms related to the management of national resources. Both processes seek a more decisive State's role regarding resource nationalization. Additionally, both revolutions, through class coalitions, opposed to social segments which gathering the majority of land and other resources. The Bolivian social mobilisation of the XXI century stands out in the country's history, because it joined privileged political opportunities to appropriate the governmental institutions. Nevertheless, even though the new institutional discourses had been renewed, between the political and social actors' underpinning domination logics, which make difficult the change the dominant hegemonic discourse for a anti hegemonic discourseof a plural production of the life of the indigenous nations, such as established in the new constitutional preamble (Tapia, 2009; González, 2013, 2014).

In this framework of both revolutions, that of 1952 and the later of 2005, exits a continuous historical exercising of precedent social struggles. Traditionally the peoples of Bolivia have sought the transformation of local domination systems and anti-Indian racism (Pati, 2009: 79). Bolivia has been a cradle for leaders who resisted. The memory of Bolivian emancipation is characterised by different leaders such as: Tupac Amaru and Tupac Katari at the beginning of the Hispanic period, Bartolina Sisa during 1780-1781, Cacique Wilka (Pablo Zarate) who characterised the republican period between 1874 and 1895, and the uprisings of Jesús Machaka in 1921, Cajes in 1914, Caquiaviri in 1918, Achakachi 1920 and 1931, and of Chayanta in 1927, among others (Mamani, 2009: 86). Furthermore is also characterised by historical memory of the against neoliberalism protests in 1983, 1985 and 1987 (Mamani, 2009: 86; Espasandín & Iglesias, 2007).

During 2005 the Bolivian mobilisation managed to institutionalise itself in the State through of the election of Evo Morales at the presidency, thus finalising the first indigenous mobilisation cycle in Latin America, being the first indigenous President of the subcontinent, he faced the materialisation of the social demands into governmental aims (Chavéz & Mokrani, 2007: 55-66). This political leader gained first election with 53,7% of the votes and has been re-elected twice: in 2009 with 64,22% and in 2014 with 60% of the votes (Svampa et al. 2010: 33). During the first government of Morales institutional transformation processes took place which later allowed the proclamation of the "Unitarian Social State of Plurinational Communitarian Rights" in the new Magna Carta signed in 2009.

The first two Morales mandates showed a political leadership oriented towards innovation in the governability, generating structural changes in the historic patterns of domination (García Linera, 2010; González, 2014). The constitutional Assembly debate which founded the New Constitution established based on the Plurinational State (2009), meant a new cycle in the relation State-nations in Bolivia (Albó/Romero, 2009; Stroebele-Gregor, 2006). During these mandates indigenous movements, trades unions, among other popular organisations promoted the formation of a new plurinational order arising from an internal political discussion which reflects the aspirations of thousands of mobilized, such as indigenous, peasants and afro Bolivians (Svampa et al. 2010). These governments have making and maintaining breaks with the traditional society which discriminated minorities for more than five centuries (Schilling Vacaflor, 2011: 9-10).

The institutionalization of these forms of plurality in Bolivia deserves special attention, as stated Sousa, they are government and citizen exercises which include pre-capitalist values, emerged before capitalism and modernity (Sousa, 2010, 2012). To understand the historical rupture achieved by the Bolivians is important to appreciate why the indigenous struggle is an ancestral struggle (González, 2006; Archila & González, 2010)[2]. The history of the indigenous in Latin-America has been marked by different resistance strategies, among these James Scott has defined the Hidden Transcripts as an form of Resistance (Scott, 2000)[3]. Through this masked resistance, these

[2] The ancestral indigenous resistance can be characterised by the following aspects: 1) it has been constant since the Conquest until today; its "communitarian" position has been expressed on the official political scenario only in some occasions, often remained as a hidden transcript, 2) it emerged from a sense of belonging and as territorial defence, 3) its common political aim is to reaffirm its autonomy and 4) the most successful strategies in this resistance exercise have been non armed (González, 2006: 87-102).

[3] James Scott analyses the relation between dominators and subordinates, starting from two different types of discourse appreciable into the power relations: public or official, motivated by the hegemonic power the elite and socially accepted as legitimate; and hidden dialogue, in which the codes, reactions, strategies and practices are expressed in the language of the dominated. This subordinate language is isolated from public spheres and official society and is deployed only in the internal sphere of the social movements or in ghettos or peripheral groups. The hidden discourse develops through subaltern practices among the oppressed and allows the creation of solidarities and fluid communication mechanisms for those who are "accepted as equals" (Scott, 2000).

collectives have undermined the subordinate role which they had historically been assigned in the sociocultural, political and economic spheres. This fact created group potentialities, which they have made more visible after the nineties, when they have being included as political actors. The indigenous struggles for the recognition of their autonomy, territory, rights and authorities, have caused deep tensions between the powerful and the oppressed (Archila & González, 2010: 148-173). Although, in many cases, all that can be identified is a relative improvement in exclusion-, but in the construction of environmental changes in the XXI century these local practices are fundamental in the construction of alternative orders based on self-management, self-development and solidarity. The last part of this chapter analyses some of these local exercises as key social practices.

One of the most significant processes in the transformation is the Constitutional Assembly debate, which represented a simultaneous confrontation of interests scenario between diverse political actors, in some cases ambivalent, which managed to put together a model of social and political change because it fundamentally retook identity elements from their aboriginal beliefs (García Linera, et al. 2010: 9-43). Among the most representative of the Constitutional Assembly's achievements, is the legal basis conceded to the "indigenous nations." The national plurality and its socio-political validity arise as a concept of reconstitution of the *ayllu*, as a local space in the reconstitution of their own forms of organisation, as well as the struggle aims for the indigenous authorities. The *ayllu* represents, in itself, the concrete social and anthropological territoriality of these communities, it symbolises the thinking for producing and living in the social life, in this sense it embodies the actual time-space form of the indigenous communities (Mamani, 2009: 94; Exeni, 2015)[4]. This return of the ayllu is also the return of the redefinition of a new social and institutional territoriality, which retakes the historical territories and revives the identity values of the "nations" (Mamani, 2009: 142). However, above all it reaffirms the importance of the local organic sphere in the constitution of truly inclusive societies.

In that sense, the plurinationality of the indigenous nations emerged constitutionally meant articulating said nations just as the *ayllu* were formerly articulated, reconstructing different levels of government (*Thankhi*) (Mamani,

[4] The *ayllu* also "directs the particular ways of realisation of land rituals to the deity "pachamama", also to other masculine and feminine deities (*achachilas*), as well in the communitarian work system (*ayni o mink'a*). In addition to this, the ayllu determines the rotation of power, under the duality of social and territorial space (*saya*), and controls the authority systems (*muyt'a*), etc." (taken from Mammani, 2009: 94).

2009; Exeni, 2015). These forms of government applied to the indigenous societies of the area *Abya Yala* or *Tawantinsuyana* before the arrival of the Spaniards. The indigenous societies recreated and organised their material and symbolic world based on the appropriation of the territory, this last is clearly evidenced in their economic and linguistic structures framed in a political autonomy exercise (Pati, 2009: 25-27). Referring to the Charchas Memorial of (1582), the governmental system of local micro-governments with different levels of power *Thankhi*, was readopted, which represents a set of procedures, principles, values and representativeness of the local communities (Mamani, 2009). The territorial structuring implied the definition of markas, a identity local delimitation of the nations (*pakajaqi*), which, in the Bolivian case has two large indigenous families: 1) *Urqusuyu* and 2) *Umasuyu* (Pati, 2009: 25-27).

In the previous perspective, the new constitution is profoundly ambitious as it institutionalises political diversity through plurinationality, which is articulated through the shared beliefs of the diverse indigenous peasant organisations which after intense struggles and debates decided to integrate with the Unitary Pact of the Constitutional Assembly (González, 2015). In this pact gathered different peasant organisations with regional or national leadership, among which are to be found: the Unique Confederation of Rural Labourers of Bolivia (CSUTCB), Federation of native and Indigenous Peasant Women, of Bolivia “Bartolina Sisa” (FNMCB-BS), the Trade Union Confederation of Colonisers of Bolivia (CSCB), the Confederation of Indigenous People of Bolivia – CIDOB, the National Council of Qullasuyu Ayllus and Markos – CONAMAQ, Coordinator of the Ethnic Communities of Santa Cruz – CPESC, Landless Workers Movement – MST, The Assembly of the Guaraní People, Centre for the ethnic and Moxos people of Beni – CPEMB (Pati, 2009: 38) and many others.

The constitutional changes implanted in the political and social system in Bolivia have ambitious aims not only for this country, but also for Latin-American reality. The plurinational State’s proposal interprets its own history, recognising different nations by their native language and in general with the strength of their own sociocultural repertory. The Plurinational State signifies the integration of the nations through of the principle of complementarity (*Chacha-Warmi*), the principle of equality in the redistribution of natural resources, as the moral and éthnic principles: *Ama Sua* (Do not steal), *Ama Llulla* (Do not lie) and *Ama Quella* (Do not be lazy) (Pati, 2009: 39). On the basis of implementation of their policies this implied making and maintaining breaks with the traditional society which discriminated against an indigenous, peasant majority such as Afro-Bolivian, and whose historical practices have been rooted, for more than five centuries, in the predominance of an exclusionary and corrupt culture. In effect, the materialisation of these transformations may be examined after various decades and it is undoubtable that today we are still in a period of structural ruptures in relation to the historically established order and above all, to the refounding of a new model of Bolivian political society.

RESOURCE NATIONALISM IN THE LATIN-AMERICAN CONTEXT

The protests against the Morales government can establish the differences between the governmental challenge to strengthen the new direction of the popularly created plurinational nation and the implemented political and economic agenda. During 2010, Morales and García Linera attempted to give sense to this new form of State assuring the combination of two governmental functions; social cohesion and the economic management, whose arguments were set out at that time by García Linera as follows:

> It is only the State which can unite the society; it is that which assumes the synthesis of the general will, which plans the strategic framework and represent the first carriage of the economic locomotive. The second is the private Bolivian investment; the third is foreign investment; the fourth is the small enterprise; the fifth, the peasant economy and the sixth, the indigenous economy. This is the strategic order in which the economy of the country has to be structured (García Linera quoted in Stefanoni, 2010: 72).

The institutionalisation of this State, arising from processes of popular mobilisation, has given rise to a mixture of opposing roles: on one hand adaptation of popular proposals to the legal structure and norms (liberal tendency), and, on the other, the communitarian process's own needs appear, in which is situated the central way of *buen vivir* (communitarian tendency). The Plurinational State has begun to found itself under two very different, almost self-exclusionary, patterns, and the institutionalised movement has not yet been able to define in which way it should take advantage of these to channel a truly alternative political project (Dávalos, 2004; García Linera, 2005; González, 2013). The aim of the Bolivian state policies for the modernisation of the country are altering the national policies in a contradictory way, above all in regard to that related with the nationalisation of natural resources and the beginning of large scale extractive processes (Betancourt et al. 2013)[5].

Through nationalisation, Bolivia acquired economic tools to strengthen the nationalist political trend established by Venezuela and later followed by Ecuador, Brazil, etc. This Bolivian State political strategy ruled constitutionally for the protection of: coca as cultural heritage (Art 384), mining and metallurgical resources (Art 369), water resources (Art 373), energy forms (Art 378), biodiversity and natural renewable resources (Art 380), the Amazonia (Art 390), protected areas (Art 385), natural forests and their soils (Art 386), the land and the territory (Art 393). With this nationalisation Latin-American governments established the constitutional conditions to protect the social function of their most strategic natural resources and appropriated the capital generated, revoking private ownership of these (García, 2005, Albó & Romero, 2009; González, 2015). The constitutional implementation of this social function breaks the domination patterns which historically conceded the administration of natural resources to private actors, in general private exploration companies and promotor and vendors of the mentioned resources. The State redefines the ownership of natural resources as strategic for the national conglomerate, which meets a social, social economic, cultural or environmental function. This multi-functionality predominates the right to individual private ownership including in regard to international legal entities. In this sense the progressive Latin-American states have become regulatory agents and active producers of goods and services, which have achieved unprecedented economic growth and with implications for global economic security (Mares, 2010; Wilson, 2015). This trend towards nationalisation of resources has a global character, but it implementation in Latin-America is different from other world regions, given that it is the only one which gambled on the social, economic and industrial transformation of its societies (Wilson, 2015: 6-9).

[5] Svampa (2012) characterises "extractivist development as "[…] the pattern of accumulation based on the overexploitation of natural resources largely, non-renewable, including the expansion of frontiers towards territories previously considered "unproductive". Thus defined, extractivism does not only include activities typically considered as such (mining and petroleum) but also others, such as, agribusiness or the production de agro fuels, which bring an extractivist logic through the consolidation of a trend towards single-products which destroy biodiversity, leading to acquisition of lands and the negative reconfiguration of vast territories" (Svampa 2012: 20).

While the progressive states have used extractivism on a large scale as means of accumulation of capital and this generates contradictory local environmental impacts with the protection of the rights of the populations and of the environment. It is also undeniable that only through this, the use of the extraction of these resources Latin-American states have achieved an economic advantage which they never had in their histories. In Latin-America from Hispanic times until the XX century, the state concession for natural resources was generally in the hands of private foreign actors (Galeano, 2003; Zanatta, 2012). A relevant immediate effect of nationalisation is the economic force it has given to the states of the subcontinent, as, in all the cases the national budget of said countries has doubled or more (Svampa, et al. 2010; Guajardo, 2012; Sabaini, et al. 2015). In this sense the nationalism at the beginning of the XXI century is a phenomenon which creates a window of opportunity for the legalisation and legitimation of new social practices, funded by an economically sound institutionalism.

In Latin-America and the Caribbean, between 2006 and 2010 exports of minerals and petroleum increased from 18.3% to 58.9%. During this period the region took up an important place such as producer of natural resources (González Molina, 2012). Between 2003 and 2015 the increase of the GDP in Bolivia rose from 7% to 82%. Economic growth climbed from 2,7% in 2002 to 4,9% in 2015. Today, in the subcontinental context it is the economy with the greatest growth. Social investment has increased from 629 million in 2005, to 1428 million during 2009, this investment is directly related to the increment of state income which in 2005 was 677 million of dollars, and during 2009 rose to 2349 million (García Linera, 2012; Sabaini et al. 2015; Guajardo, 2012). This government has promoted the industrialisation of metallurgical factories such as Huani, Vito, Corocero and Colas, additionally it has built the Campo Grande LPG Plant, the Chaco gas separation plant and the Chapare thermoelectric Plant (García Linera, 2012; Strobele-Gregor, 2015).

Currently Bolivia possesses 90% of the world lithium reserves. Nevertheless, exploitation difficulties do not make this a privileged investment area. In the year 2014 the discovery of mineral resource deposits by China, which became an important producer country, this fact led to a fall in prices for these resources (Fues & Ye, 2015). The natural resource exploration projections continue in the region of the Middle East and North Africa as the most privileged supply zones, followed by Russia and China (Stanislaw, 2009). Therefore Latin-America holds an uncertain place in the world resource market. Each of the progressive states seeks integration with world value chains, with the confusion and disapproval of certain sectors of society for which economic progress has an overwhelmingly devastating effect on the environment, communities, cultures and their traditional means of appropriation of territory.

Despite certain institutional advances, the constitutional reforms of the nationalism of strategic resources are double edged: on one side it has achieved the initiation of part of the previously generated social mobilisation processes objectives, but on the other, having done so before consolidating a social consensus has caused strong social polarisation processes, between those who traditionally had social power, and strongly criticise the decision to create an indigenous state[6] which questions the devastating impact of the extraction processes, among other effects of the new governments (Svampa, 2012; Betancourt, 2015; Betancourt et al. 2013). In the national sphere, the sectors which traditionally held power, tried to revert to the historical pattern of domination and delegitimise the processes of change (González, 2013; Schilling-Vacaflor, 2011). In local and international spheres the environmental movements negatively evaluated the State management in relation to resource nationalisation, considering that said management maintained the modern colonial perspective of accumulation of wealth and dispossession of the territory (Betancourt et al. 2013; Porto – Gonzalves & Betancourt, 2013).

The resource "prosperity" of the progressive governments with high environmental impacts has led to certain sectors of the society losing trust in the new political processes and to doubt about their ability to mediate between economic growth, the longed-for social redistribution, and at the same time, the respect for the cultural traditions and the well-being of the local communities (Besheim, 2015; Besheim et al. 2015). The value chains of the electronic components market and other markets connected to mineral consumption are developing accentuating inequalities in the environmental conflicts (Dientz, 2014). This inequality is reaffirmed in the continuous inequitable distribution of the environmental risks in contrast to the economic benefits, in access to the resources, their distribution and use (Dientz, 2014).

[6] In the political plane and particularly, in the pro constituent unitary pact can be observed two clear positions in relation with the State: on one hand, katarism with an ideological tendency to integrate the Indians into the "global society" through political participation in pluricultural democracy, whilst, on the other, Indianism emerged as a more radical ethnocentric ideology of distancing from the State (Pati, 2009: 20). In this last aspect there are political sectors which seek to develop a role of authority in a new sense "organisational", "provider", without including the State, as is referred to by Mammani "the slogan of the *Jach'a Karangas* nation is "it is not that the state give us a hand, but it take its hands off us"" (Mammani, 2009: 143).

Resource nationalism has generated undesirable effects for the consumer countries, such as: price volatility, increases in taxes and royalties, etc. These national policies have been considered somewhat aggressive in terms of the transnational intersectoral relations, as the business sectors dependent on the production of natural resources want to increase their productivity assuring price stability, increase their profits lowering costs as much as possible (Günther Hilpert & Mildner, 2013). The governability of this nationalism occurs in midst of confrontation dynamics between heterogeneous actors with ambivalent interests. There are also contradictions when defining the roles in the environmental governance of donor countries, industrialized consumer countries and developing countries (Simon, 2011). Hence, global multilevel environmental governance moves between the socio-economical struggles of the states which do not balance between economic growth and environmental sustainability, besides the tensions of the local communities who distrust the governmental decisions (Besheim et al. 2015; Shreuers et al. 2009). Some analysts suggest specific support for the governments of developing countries which face high rates of poverty, indigence and inequality simultaneously with commitments to environmental sustainability (Fues & Ye, 2015).

In light of the previous, from the environmental governance point of view, the integration between different sectors with ambivalent goals should reach a plan which overcomes the ratification of the agreements, which proposes sustainable models that bring stability and technological independence to developing countries. Currently in Latin-America, the countries which have implemented the resource nationalism increased by more than 40% their GDPs and even though there is a greater economic capacity, there remains a high technological dependence when exploring, extracting, and commercialising the resources which allows advancement towards the intersectoral integration with sustainable development (Sabaini et al. 2015; Jordan & Huitema, 2014). Today, Bolivia is the biggest producer of lithium in the world, but lacks the technology to extract and commercialise this mineral productively.

To conclude this discussion on the understanding of the effects of the resource nationalism in nations, the State and the citizenship in the XXI century, it is fundamental to reflect on the of the comprehension of the global territorialisation dynamics which define segmented spaces for symbologies of power between those included and excluded[7] (Rodríguez & Aponte, 2008:

[7] Historically the State besides local peripheral actors have been articulated following a modern colonial domination logic; however local spaces are dynamic, capable of creating and redefining their space and culture, struggling for legitimation and legalisation of new fields of domain.

128). In Bolivia although an essential place is constitutionally guaranteed to nature in the lives of its nations, State greater participation in the administration of natural resources has not assured a greater compliance and implementation of environmental policies (Gross & Foyer, 2010; De Leon Naviero, 2013); on the contrary, particularly after 2014, governmental policies have given priority to modernisation criteria which conflict with local communities' decisions (Gamboa, 2010). This is even more relevant on observing the contradictions of the promised decentralization as a transformation process in the Bolivian reality (Exeni, 2015).

The constitutionally proposed decentralisation in Bolivia has had great obstacles since its establishment (Stefanoni & Svampa, 2010; Exeni, 2015). During 2009 the governmental decisions in front of the differences with the opposition appear to be much closer authoritarianism or centralism, than to decentralization (Gamboa, 2010). Furthermore in 2009 the Plurinational State constitutionally established the autonomy of the different types of constitutionally instituted territories, this to say, Tierras Comunitarias de Orígen - TCO[8], the different indigenous territories (Chimán, Multiétnico, Originario Campesino, Pluriétnico, Parque National Isiboro-Securé, among others), the Indigenous Territorial Entities Native Peasants, in addition to the autonomy at departmental, regional, municipal spheres (Albó & Romero, 2009).

Despite the established decentralisation at constitutional level, this came into conflict with the governmental exercise when it came to granting administrative independence to the regions (Exeni, 2015). The departments with greater economic and productive capacity have permanently opposed the political project of the MAS led by Evo Morales. Particularly, the Santa Cruz department has, at different times, led independence movements against central government. There were initiatives which were followed by Pando, Tarija and Beni, whose political project is centred on strengthening the mestiza and white classes, and their interests (Schilling-Vacaflor 2011, Espansandín & Iglesias, 2007)[9]. During the Constitutional Assembly the topic of capital caused fracturing processes and direct confrontation. The new Constitution established administrative decentralisation by various legals measures,

---

[8] TCO is a Bolivian designation given to autonomous and communally owned indigenous lands.

[9] The regional division of Bolivia by departments is the following: Cuchisaca, La Paz, Cochabamba, Oruro, Potosí, Tarija, Santa Cruz, Beni and Pando. According to the National Statistics Institute, The percentage growth of GDP by Department between 1989 and 2011 is enunciated as follows: Cuchisaca (2,1%), La Paz (3,2%), Cochabamba (3,3%), Oruro (4,2%), Potosí (4,3%), Tarija (7,5%), Santa Cruz (4,4%), Beni (2,8%) and Pando (5,1%) (Schilling-Vacaflor 2011: 7-8).

nevertheless, facing the of separatist autonomy positions of the Santa Cruz Department, the government has taken more centralist and hierarchical decisions that progressives, maintaining they prioritise the interests of the nations before those of the eastern enterprise class (González, 2013). In May of 2008 the Santa Cruz department held a referendum to legitimise its political objective of autonomy from the central government, this referendum with a "yes" at 86%, but the central government declared the regional initiative illegal. This was the high point of social polarisation and political violence between the government and the opposition (Mamani, 2011; García Linera, 2010). In September of the same year there were protests and taking of state institutions by the opposition, and in Pando, 18 representatives were massacred (Svampa, 2010).

Due to these discrepancies in the way how Bolivian Plurinational State is choosing its economic, social and cultural models and structures, which range between constitutional decentralisation and centralism, what remained undeveloped is the legitimation of the popular plurinational nation in relation to the new policies implemented by the State. Dávalos, an intellectual critic of the last years of Morales government, assures that the state structures have not generated an epistemological matrix from the ancestral knowledge present in the political practices of the indigenous communities. This author affirms that in the Latin-American subcontinent there are more than 35 million indigenous people, of around 400 ethnic groups and this, the renovation of the Plurinational State is a question related to the creation, recreation, recuperation and reconstitution of these groups' knowledge (Dávalos, 2004). From this critical perspective, another autor, Tapia also questions the type of representation exercised by the governments of Evo assuring that these reply to a political alliance and not an organic coalition, as it has not brought about a structural transformation regarding the reproduction of property or in relation with the economic structures. Hence, Bolivia needs a change against the structures which favour the concentration of the property, needs to complete the particular agrarian historical temporalities which corresponds to the thinking of peasant and communitarian societies, "an autonomous participation of anticapitalistic subjectivities which build on the conflict, emancipation experiences" (Tapia, 2009: 6).

Finally, an illustrative case of the contradictions around decentralisation of the Morales government, but also about the complexity of ambivalent interests is the case of the National Park Isiboro Sécure–TIPNIS. During 2011 the bolivian government decide to build a motorway which connects the Park–TIPNIS to the north with the capital to the south east with Brazil, this fact caused the reaction of indigenous, who protested against the government (Betancourt et al. 2013). In 2011 there were almost 1.000 protestors walking for weeks towards The Paz, the State capital, to express their opposition. This park is an important natural reserve in Bolivia, created in 1965. From 1990, the TIPNIS held the double status of Protected Area (PA) and Originary communitarian Land - TCO. The indigenous nations of this place are made up of the Moxeña Trinitaria Nation of the mojeños trinitarios, the Tsimán Chimán Nation of the tsimanes and the Yuracaré Nation of the yucarares. Late colonisation processes of the arrival of quechuas and aimaras groups allowed them to undertook private productive activities in the zone (Porto-Gonzalves & Betancourt, 2013; Betancourt et al. 2013).

The president, Evo Morales, in 2009 undertook a redressing legal process on TIPNIS park to reduce the indigenous property titles, consequently the conceding hectares deeded to 1.091.656 hectares, when initially the park covered 1.236.296 hectares (García Linera, 2012; Betancourt et al. 2013). This legal process also bounded the construction of new settlements. The protestors argued that constitutionally the government should firstly consult the communities, moreover the development of this project implied the de-territorialisation of their native populations. In the park territories take place different kind of conflicts: socio-spatial forestry, socio-spatial pecuniary, socio-spatial for the coca, for the gas and the petroleum, in the same manner socio-spatial for the agriculture. Even is important to highlight that this area conserves a biomass of 500–700 species per hectare (Porto-Gonzalves & Betancourt, 2013: 23-24). Thus, the importance of the TIPNIS conflict is based on two interrelated points. The first one is that the construction of this infrastructure integrates the area into an economic regional dynamic. The second is that the government aim's conceding the exploration and exploitation of the resources is to accelerate sales rates, regardless of the space time temporalities typical of the area, this don't consider the territoriality and the territorialisation of the local communities[10].

Between the protestors against this project two facets are notable. On one side is the traditional opposition to the government build up of the elite belonging the ex-governing class and which value this conflict a potential destabilisation agent for the current government. On other side, the indigenous communities who do not accept the construction of the motorway, as for more than 186 years of residence in this area, they have used rivers as mean

[10] There is no territory without territoriality (way of life, feeling/thinking the space), which has undergone a process of territorialisation in which a power relation take place (Porto – Gonzalves and Betancourt, 2013: 9).

transport (Betancourt, 2015). The governmental motive for creating this infrastructure is related to the possibility of becoming the principal extractor of Lithium, a mineral found in the parklands, which has a strategic value in the world market of non-renewable natural resources.

The State has reported the negative influence by the NGO as facilitators of transnational control of biotechnology and biodiversity in the park[11], in addition to this has assured that the indigenous communities do not have territorial control of the zone, whilst the colonising communities dominate 41% of the cattle farming. The Bolivian State will no way consider a shared principle of sovereignty in this zone and argues that the motorway length is 306 kilometres, from which only 16 km needs to be built, and 56,6 km belong to traditional paths which need been substitute by roads (García Linera, 2012: 67-69). The Bolivian presidency asserts that extractivism doesn't represent the main aim of this government, thus its real objective is to achieve the communitarisation of the production of the material life in the society (García Linera, 2012, 2012: 105). Linera, as a sly politician, assures that there is no historical evidence that extractives projects are more harmful that the industrial capitalistic projects, then for him the safeguard the fair distribution of the resources corresponds to the local communities (García Linera, 2012: 79-96).

ENVIRONMENTAL CHANGES AND *BUEN VIVIR* MODELS

The configuration of the energy resource market power relations shows the basis of a globalised capitalist system focussed on increasing capital flows in the global value chains, either using technological innovation. The capitalism tries to determine the form of organisation and of understanding of the space; whilst the State represses or facilitates the national imaginaries defined criteria of insecurity/security, dominant flows, the exoticism of the otherness (Rodríguez & Aponte, 2008: 137). Nevertheless, despite the on-going existence of this double dynamic, there are spaces of political, territorial and identitary differentiation, although they are raised on peripheral spaces, they develop also a cohesive and/or differentiating function of the above nominated imaginaries (Escobar, 2010). This is the case of the temporary

[11] This park is made up of diverse ecosystems: cloud forest, humid forest, Andean river forest, pluvial piedmont forests, seasonally moist basal forests, palmares wetlands, flood plains, cypercíceas wetlands and lakes (García Linera, 2012: 36-37).

space constructions of the indigenous communities, afro-descendants, peasants who for centuries have used their own practices of survival even as taking delight of own life experiences.

Capitalist modernisation, based on economic growth, continues structuring centres of world power; however the solutions to climatic change do not consider a reduction in the emissions of contaminant gases through of the restructuring of modern life (Sorda et al. 2012). The States, the business sectors and inhabitants of the major cities are not willing to give up the comforts of progress (air conditioning, heating, lifts, escalators, indiscriminate use of cars, hot water, etc.), at the same time industry producers are responsible of 80% of this contamination, but they are only willing to pay environmental taxes in retribution for the damaging effects of their productive activities (Bettini & Karaliotas, 2013).

Even though, the day to day symptoms of environmental changes show that all around the world there are local people, networks and associations who seek alternatives to overcome the current environmental and social crises. The importance of this search is understanding that these are spaces where ancestral knowledge has taken up the public sphere (Escobar, 2010: 189). From this perspective the Bolivian constitution established a wider conceptual cultural world regarding nature, in this sense historical communitarian experiences can offer alternative uses of nature (Escobar, 2010: 217-219). The Bolivian constitution as a process reflects the strong pressures of social mobilisation demanding the priority place of nature as a common good. In the past, a fundamental principle which led to the “Gas War” and “Water War,” mobilisations in Bolivia was the recognition of these resources not as public but as a belonging part of the national identity (Chávez/Mokrani, 2007).

From this perspective nature is understood as “culturally constructed”[12]: “History suggests a deep interconnection between different reality levels or domains: biophysical, human and supernatural” (Escobar, 2010:133). Therefore ancestral knowledge of indigenous and afro-descendants communities’ understand humanity in interdependence with nature. Both communities structure their reality with categories such as top-down, divine-human, inside-outside, common beliefs–the others (Escobar, 2010: 134-140).

[12] According to Arturo Escobar, political ecology is an interdisciplinary field which includes many disciplines (geography, anthropology, ecology, political science, ecological economy, environmental history, historical ecology, development studies, science and technology), moreover encompasses different theoretical areas (liberal, Marxist post-structural theory, feminist theory, phenomenology, postcolonial theory, complexity and natural science approaches, such as landscape ecology and conservation biology) (Escobar, 2010: 36-37).

In their practices are envisaged as de-colonial relations of nature, promoting the interrelationship of natural ecological, economic and cultural processes, this means a new reformulation of conservation, of sustainability and of production, which implies also recognising other socio-natural worlds (Escobar, 2010: 133-182). Hence "Sustainability" may become an "otherness" project through different worlds and knowledge" (Escobar, 2010: 172).

This perspective of knowledge brings understanding from the constructivist dialectical Marxist approach applied to non-western models. The constructivism accepts the connectivity between the subject and the object of knowledge, thinking from a scientific perspective and also from a materialistic perspective, in this sense reality is socially constructed. The dialectical Marxist constructivism proposes the constant transformation of social reality as a product of conflicts and power, consequently under an ecological perspective, exist the dialectic dynamic between the organisms and the environment (Escobar, 2010: 142-152). In social terms this dialectic also applies to the care of the environment, in this sense the example of the communities local based, on their location they have internalised ecological and cultural conditions in their social relations and in the productive systems of their societies (Escobar, 2010: 171).

In light of the above, the new Plurinational State has the challenge to integrate the shared indigenous communities' values into the national and international political systems. In this way, it is correct to re-evaluate that which was affirmed in my previous publications about the challenges of the Bolivian State (González, 2013, 2014). Currently it is more accurate to consider that, the main point of analysis of the coming years should not be address on determining if the State institutionally continues using a Liberal perspective relegating the communitarian one. It would be better to focuses on the implementation processes of the new policies, to determine which communitarian's concepts have become part of the nations legacy. This means which have become legitimate and effective in the local practices developed during of construction of the new social order. This in the system of multilateral governance favours the indigenous environmental dimension as a starting point to tackle common problems on the world agenda. In this regard, the current chapter concludes its reflection on the nationalism resource and the environmental changes in Bolivia, highlighting some elements which can contribute to this analysis.

The Bolivian nations are predominately indigenous; their cosmo-vision conceives integration between polarities. Lo "communitarian" in the political construction of the Bolivian plurinational State means the interdependence of the different, even if exists polarisation between them. This inclusive logic can be explain under the concept of harmony in the parity, present in nature. According to Estermann, "existence" in Andean philosophy is not represented in the subject and object relation, but in the reaction of this relation, thus relationality with the others, with the outside sphere represents the centre of the world-state and of the self knowledge (Estermann, 1998). In this way, this logic differs from the logic of modern rationality in which the subject converts itself in the same world, subject himself creates the reality. The indigenous collective identity is based on the relationality between heterogeneities and on the relationality in diversity (Lajó, 2006). In this way, a person exists in the measure which relates with the world outside itself, recognizing world as an alive entity (Estermann, 1998: 201-206). So, indigenous thinking recognize other culture, as a possibility of recognizing this other culture transcendence, therefore this approach allows continuous syncretism, instead a differentiation regarding cultural diversity. This way of thinking does not recognise individualistic moral, but accepts a collective life construction. The mentioned Cosmo vision is present in the beliefs, values, norms and social practices of the Andean communities. Its creates collective cultural frameworks, through which solidarities are transmitted, as well as temporalities of their action cycles and other components which make up the constant syncretism of indigenous identity (Archila & González, 2010: 148-173).

In the political arena all the indigenous Latin-American movements are expressed in communitarian actions, which cannot be equated with the collective actions of other social movements, as they do not orient their collective value from abstract criteria for the common good, but acquire their shared social sense according to the cultural and historical values of their own conditions. The Nuclear Communitarian Actions condense the communitarian sense of the political process, recouping the sense of the common history of resistance and reaffirming the values which underpin their common identity: preservation of territory, autonomy, unity and own culture (Archila & González, 2010: 148-173). These actions are sustained in the life values and dignity of the communities, besides their ancestral and originary land's rights. In this measure the defence of land, such as other natural resources, represents a reason for mobilisation, perhaps the element which fuels the internal cohesion and the external struggle for their defence, such as happened in Bolivia during the Water War and the Gas War.

For Rappaport actions such as the recuperation of land - or of other resources belonging to the communities - represent three key points for to the construction of a common identity into a movement: firstly, the land means the collective reincorporation as possibility to amend their history, furthermore reaffirms their collective feelings and common ancestors; secondly, shows the strengthening of their Council's authority; and thirdly, refers to the articulation of the forefathers spirits to their current reality (Rappaport, 2005: 27-33). The communitarian power is of vital importance, given that the policy reaffirms the re-flexibility of its members, finding negotiation points with their adversaries and constructing consensus.

CONCLUSION

Undoubtedly there are complex tensions surrounding the institutionalisation of the plurinational Bolivian State, these tensions will sight this country at least during the beginning of 21st century. Even though the new institutional discourses had been renewed with the constitution of 2009, there are underpinning domination logics between the political and social actors, which have rooted for more than five centuries in the predominance of an exclusionary and corrupt culture. The implementation of new policies implies making and maintaining breaks with the historically established order. In effect, the materialisation of these transformations should be examined after various decades. Today is still a period of structural ruptures, besides the implementation of a new pattern domains.

In Bolivia although an essential place is constitutionally guaranteed to nature in the lives of its nations; State administration of natural resources has not assured a greater compliance and implementation of environmental policies. On the contrary, the last ten years confirm that the Bolivian state is concern of developing policies for the modernisation, in a contradictory way, above all in regard to those related with the development of large scale extractive processes. The new Plurinational State has the challenge to integrate the shared indigenous communities' values into the national and international political systems. Bolivian constitution established a wider conceptual cultural world regarding nature, in this sense historical communitary experiences can offer alternative uses of nature as a common good. The multilateral governance system is beginning to recognize the indigenous environmental behaviours as a starting point to tackle common problems on the climate agenda.

From the indigenous Cosmo-vision recognising other culture necessarily implies understanding its transcendence, therefore the indigenous approach of knowledge regarding cultural diversity allows a continuous syncretism, instead differentiation between cultures. Dávalos assures that the new state structures need to generated an epistemological matrix from the ancestral knowledge present in the political practices of the indigenous communities. In the same way, Tapia recommends an organic coalition as representation principle to bringing a structural transformation regarding the reproduction of property or in relation with the economic structures. Hence, Bolivia needs structures able to recognize of the own agrarian historical time of their communitarian societies.

ACKNOWLEDGMENTS

This article belongs to the research project entitled: "Governability in Latin America: plurinational constitutions and "resource nationalism" in the XXI century," which is financed by an interinstitutional cooperation agreement between the Political and Social Sciences Department of the University of Bologna (Italy) and the Institute of Socio-Historical Studies Fray Alonso de Zamora of the University Santo Tomás (Colombia).

REFERENCES

Albó, Xavier and Romero, Carlos (2009). *Autonomías Indígenas en la realidad boliviana y su constitución* (Indigenous autonomy in Bolivian reality and its Constitution). La Paz: GTZ.

Archila, Mauricio and González, Nidia Catherine (2010). *Movimiento Indígena caucano: historia y política* (Cauca Indigenous Movement: History and Politics). Tunja: Santo Tomás University Press.

Besheim, Marianne (2015). Reviewing the Post-2015 Sustainable Development Goals and Partnerships, A Proposal for a Multi-level Review at the High level Political Forum. SWP Berlin. [http://www.swp-berlin.org/fileadmin/contents/products/research_papers/2015_RP01_bsh.pdf]. *Research Paper RP 01, SWP Berlin.*

Besheim, Marianne, Lokken, Hadda, Aus Dem Moore, Nils, Pintér, Lászlo and Rickels, Wilfried (2015). Measuring Sustainable Development: How can Science Contribute to Realizing the SDGs? [http://www.swp-berlin.org/fileadmin/contents/products/arbeitspapiere/Beisheim-et-al_WorkingPaper_MeasuringSD.pdf]. *Research Paper FG 8, SWP Berlin.*

Betancourt, Milson (2015). Ejes de la IIRSA: la maquina se friega pero el territorio queda (IIRSA axes: the machine is scrubbed but the territory remains). [https://www.youtube.com/watch?v=sX4zA8QxnmM]. *Documentales you tube. Entrevistas de campo Julio/Agosto 2013* (You Tube documentaries. Field interviews July/August 2013).

Betancourt, Milson, Hurtado, Lina M and Porto Gonçalves, Carlos Walter (2013). *Tensiones territoriales y políticas públicas de desarrollo en la Amazonia* (Territorial tensions and public policy development in the Amazon). Buenos Aires: CLACSO.

Bettini, Giovanni and Karaliotas, Lazaro (2013). Exploring the limits of peak oil: naturalising the political, de-politicising energy. *The Geographical Journal.* Vol. 179, No. 4, 331-341.

Chávez, Patricia and Mokrani, Dunia (2007). Los movimientos sociales en la asamblea constituyente, hacia la reconfiguración de la política (Social movements in the constituent assembly, to the reconfiguration of politics). In: E.E. Svampa, Maristella and Stefanoni, Pablo, *Bolivia, Memoria, insurgencia y movimientos sociales* (Bolivia, Memory, insurgency and social movements). CLACSO.

Cuscicanqui Rivera, Silvia (1984). *Oprimidos pero no vencidos* (Oppressed but not defeated). La Paz, Hisbol – CSUTCB.

Dávalos, Pablo (2004). Movimientos Indígenas en América Latina, el derecho a la palabra (Indigenous movements in Latin America, the right to speak). In: E.E. Dávalos, Pablo (Ed.), *Pueblos Indígenas, Estado y Democracia* (Indigenous peoples, State and Democracy), pp. 17-33. Buenos Aires: CLACSO.

De León Naviero, Omar (2013). Dualismo Productivo y construcción de otro desarrollo en Bolivia (Productive dualism and build another development in Bolivia). In: E.E. Vidal, Gregorio, Guillen, Arturo and Déniz, José (Ed.), *América Latina Como construir el desarrollo hoy*? (Latin America and build development today?) pp. 291-310. México: Fondo de Cultura Económica (Mexico: Bottom of Economic Culture).

Dientz, Kristina (2014). Researching Inequialities from a socio ecological Perspective. [http://www.iai.spk-berlin.de/fileadmin/dokumentenbibliothek/desigualdades/workingpapers/74_WP_Dietz_Online.pdf] *Working paper N. 74.*

Escobar, Arturo (2010). *Territorios de diferencia, Lugar, movimientos, redes, vida* (Unlike territories, Location, movements, networks, life). Popayán: Samava Printers.

Estermann, Josef (1998). *Filosofía Andina, estudio intercultural de la sabiduria autoctona andina* (Andean philosophy, cultural study of Andean indigenous knowledge). Quito: Abya Yala Press.

Exeni, José Luis (2015). Bolivia: las autonomías indígenas frente al estado plurinacional (Bolivia: indigenous autonomy against the multinational state). In: E.E. Lang, Miriam, Cevallos, Belén and López, Claudia (Eds.): *Como transformar? Instituciones y cambio social en America Latina y Europa*, (How to transform? Institutions and Social Change in Latin America and Europe) pp. 145-190. Colombia: Abya Yala Press/Rosa Luxemburgo Foundation.

Espasandín López, Jesus and Iglesias Turrión, Pablo (Eds.) (2007). *Bolivia en movimiento, Accion colectiva y poder político* (Bolivia moving, collective action and political power) España: El Viejo Topo Publisher.

Fues, Thomas and Ye, Jiang (Eds.) (2015). The United Nations Post-2015 Agenda for Global Development: Perspectives from China and Europe. [https://www.die-gdi.de/uploads/media/Studies_84.pdf]. DIE.

Galeano, Eduardo (2003). *Las venas abiertas de América latina* (Open Veins of Latin America). México: Siglo XXI Publishers.

Gamboa, Franco (2010). Transformaciones constitucionales en Bolivia (Constitutional changes in Bolivia). *Colombia Internacional*, N. 71, 151-188.

Gandarillas, M., Tahbub, M. and Rodríguez, G. (2008). *Nacionalización de los hidrocarburos en Bolivia. La lucha de un pueblo por sus recursos naturales* (Nationalization of hydrocarbons in Bolivia. The struggle of a people for its natural resources). Barcelona: Icaria.

García Linera, Alvaro (2005). *Estado multinacional. Una propuesta democrática para la extinción de la exclusión de las naciones indias* (Multinational state. A Democratic proposal to extinguish the exclusion of the Indian nations) La Paz: Malatesta Press.

García Linera, Alvaro (2010). El estado en transición. Bloque de poder y punto de bifurcación (The state in transition. Power block and branching point). In: Álvaro García Linera (Ed.) *El Estado. Campo de Lucha* (The state. Battlefield). La Paz: Muela del Diablo, 2010.

García Linera, Alvaro (2012). *Geopolitica de la Amazonía, poder haciendal – patrimonial y acumulación capitalista* (Geopolitics of the Amazon, to haciendal - equity and capital accumulation) La Paz: Vicepresidencia del Estado plurinacional boliviano (La Paz: Bolivian Vice multinational state).

González Molina, Rodolfo Iván (2012). Desarrollo económico de América Latina y las integraciones regionales del siglo XXI (Latin American economic development and regional integration of the XXI century). *Ecos de Economía*, [http://www.scielo.org.co/pdf/ecos/v16n35/v16n35a6.pdf], Volume number 35-16.

González, Milena (2015). *Trayectorias del derecho a la propiedad en Bolivia* (Paths property rights in Bolivia). Bogotá: Editorial UD/Dialogos.

González, Nidia Catherine (2014). Democrazia e pluralità, da diritti etnici a costituzioni plurinazionali (1991-2012) (Democracy and plurality, from ethnic rights toconstitutions plurinational (1991-2012)). *Rivista di Studi Iberoamericani: Confluenze* (Journal of Studies Iberoamerican: Confluenze), Vol. 6, Nº 2, 29-38.

González, Nidia Catherine (2013). Sfide e tensioni nello Stato plurinazionale boliviano (Challenges and tensions in the Plurinational State of Bolivia). In: *Dallo stato del bienestar allo stato del buen vivir* (From welfare state to weel beeng State) Bologna: Filodiritto Editore, pp. 136-155.

González, Nidia Catherine (2006). *Resistencia indígena, alternativa en medio del conflicto* (Indigenous resistence, alternative means of conflict) Cali: Javeriana Press.

Gross, Christian and Foyer, Jean (Eds) (2010). ¿Desarrollo con identidad? Gobernanza económica indígena, siete estudios de caso (Development with identity? Indian economic governance, seven case studies) Quito: FLACSO.

Guajardo Soto, Guillermo (2012). América Latina: ¿zona mixta o continente perdido en las últimas cuatro décadas?. (Latin America: mixed zone or continent lost in the last four decades?) *Economía y Sociedad* (Economy and Society). [http://www.scielo.org.mx/scielo.php?pid=S1665-85742012000200002&script=sci_arttext].

Günther Hilpert, Hanns and Mildner, Stormy-Annika (2013). Nationale Alleingänge oder internationale Kooperation? Analyse und Vergleich der Rohstoffstrategien der G20-Staaten (Unilateral national or international cooperation? Analysis and comparison of commodity strategies of the G20 countries). [http://www.swp-berlin.org/fileadmin/contents/products/studien/2013_S01_hlp_mdn.pdf]. *Research Paper*. Ein Kooperationsprojekt der Stiftung Wissenschaft und Politik (SWP) und der Bundesanstalt für Geowissenschaften und Rohstoffe (BGR) (A joint project of the Stiftung Wissenschaft und Politik (SWP) and the Federal nstitute for Geosciences and Natural Resources (BGR).

Jordan Andrew and Huitema (2014). Policy innovation in a changing climate: Sources, patterns and effects. *Global Environmental Change*, Volume 29: 387-394, [http://www.sciencedirect.com/science/article/pii/S0959378014001605].

Klein, Herbert (1969). *Parties and political change in Bolivia 1880-1956*. Cambridge: University Press.

Lajó, Javier (2006). *Qhapaq Ñan: La ruta de la sabiduría Inca* (Qhapaq Ñan: The route of the Inca wisdom). Quito: Ediciones Abya Yala.

Mammani, Pablo (2011). Estado Plurinacional y autonomías desiguales (Plurinational State and unequal autonomies), *Revista Willka*, No. 3, 31-67.

Mammani, Pablo (2009). Reconstitución y cartografía del poder ayllu (Reconstitution and mapping of power ayllu). In: E.E. Pati, Pelagio, Mamani, Pablo, Quispe, Norah, *Sistematización de experiencias de movimientos indígenas en Bolivia* (Systematization of indigenous movements in Bolivia), pp. 75-152. La Paz: UMSA.

Mares, David (2012). Resource nationalism and energy security in Latin America. [www.bakerinstitute.org/publications/EFpub-MaresResourceNationalismWorkPaper-012010.pdf]. *Working Paper*. James Baker III. Institute of public policy, Rice University.

Mires, Fernando (1988). Bolivia: la revolución obrera que fue campesina (Bolivia: the workers' revolution that was peasant). In: E.E. Mires, Fernando, *La rebelión permanente: las revoluciones sociales en América Latina* (The permanent rebellion: social revolutions in Latin America). México: Siglo XXI, 158-223.

Pati, Pelagio (2009). La plurinacionalidad y el cambio en la estructura del Estado Boliviano (Plurinationality and change in the structure of the Bolivian State). In: E.E. Pati, Pelagio, Mamani, Pablo, Quispe, Norah, *Sistematización de experiencias de movimientos indígenas en Bolivia* (Systematization of indigenous movements in Bolivia), 15-76. La Paz: UMSA.

Porto-Gonzalves Carlos Walter and Betancourt, Milson (2013). Encrucijadas latinoamericanas en Bolivia: el conflict del TIPNIS y sus implicaciones civilizatorias (Latin American Crossroads in Bolivia: TIPNIS conflict and civilizational implications). [http://www.cedib.org/wp-content/uploads/2013/05/El-conflicto-del-TIPNIS-y-sus-implicaciones.pdf].

Sabaíni, Juan Carlos, Jiménez, Juan Pablo and Morán, Dalmiro (2015). El impacto fiscal de la explotación de los recursos naturales no renovables en los países de América Latina y el Caribe (The fiscal impact of the exploitation of non-renewable natural resources in Latin America and the Caribbean). [http://repositorio.cepal.org/bitstream/handle/11362/38235/S1500128_es.pdf] CEPAL.

Schilling-Vacaflor, Almut (2011). Bolivia's New Constitution: Towards Participatory Democracy and Political Pluralism?. *European Review of Latin American and Caribbean Studies*, No. 90, 3-22.

Schreurs, Miranda A., Vandeveer, Stacy and Selin, Henrik (Eds). (2009). *Transatlantic Environment and Energy Politics: Comparative and International Perspectives*. Farnham, UK: Ashgate Press.

Scott, James (2000). *Los dominados y el arte de la resistencia* (Domination and the Arts of Resistance). México: Ediciones Era.

Simon, Nils (2011). International Environmental Governance for the 21st Century, Challenges, Reform Processes and Options for Action on the Way to Rio 2012. [https://www.swp-berlin.org/fileadmin/contents/products/research_papers/2011_RP01_sin_ks.pdf]. *Research Paper RP 01*, SWP Berlin.

Sorda, Giovanni, Banse, Martin and Kemfert, Claudia (2012) An overview of biofuel policies across the world. *Energy Policy*, 6(1). 38, 37-52.

Sousa Santos, Boaventura (2010). *Refundación del Estado en América Latina. Perspectivas desde una epistemología del sur* (Re-founding the State in Latin America. Perspectives from a South epistemology). Bogotá: Siglo XXI Editores, Universidad de los Andes.

Sousa Santos, Boaventura (2012). *De las dualidades a las ecologías* (From dualities to ecologies). La Paz: REMTE-Red Boliviana de Mujeres Transformando la Economía (La Paz: Bolivian REMTE - Network of Women Transforming the Economy).

Stefanoni, Pablo (2007). Las tres fronteras de la revolución de Evo Morales, Neodesarrollismo, desicionismo y multiculturalismo (The three border Evo Morales Revolution, neodevelopmentalism, desicionismo and multiculturalism). In: E.E. Svampa, Maristella and Stefanoni, Pablo: *Bolivia, Memoria, insurgencia y movimientos sociales* (Bolivia, Memory, insurgency and social movements). Buenos Aires: CLACSO.

Stroebele-Gregor, Juliana (2005). Bolivien – Auf dem Weg zur Neugestaltung der Demokratie (Bolivia - Towards the redesign of democracy). En: *Krisenregionen in Lateinamerika, weingartener Lateinamerika-Gespraeche 2005* (Crisis regions in Latin America, Latin America Weingartener Talks 2005). Hamburg: Institut fuer Iberoamerika-kunde, pp. 229-250.

Stroebele-Gregor, Juliana (2015). Desigualdades estructurales en el aprovechamiento de un recurso estratégico, la economía global del litio y el caso de Bolivia (Structural inequalities in harnessing a strategic resource, the global lithium economy and the Bolivian case). [http://www.iai.spk-berlin.de/fileadmin/dokumentenbibliothek/desigualdades/workingpapers/WP-79-Stroebele--Gregor-Online.pdf] *Working Paper No. 79.*

Stanislaw, Joseph (2009). *Resource nationalism, the global scramble for energy and the need for mutual interdependence.* Deloitte Center for Energy solutions.

Svampa, Maristella, Stefanoni, Pablo and Fornillo, Bruno (2010). *Debatir Bolivia, perspectivas de un proyecto de descolonización* (Discuss Bolivia, prospects of decolonization project), Buenos Aires: Taurus.

Svampa, Maristella (2012). Consenso de los commodities, giro ecoterritorial y pensamiento crítico en América Latina (Consensus of commodities, ecoterritorial turn and critical thinking in Latin America). In: Svampa et al. (Eds.), *Movimientos socioambientales en América Latina*, OSAL, Año XIII (Social and environmental movements in Latin America, NPOs, Year XIII) N. 32, pp. 15-38.

Tapia, Luis (2009). *La coyuntura de la autonomía relativa del Estado* (The situation of relative autonomy of the state). La Paz: CLACSO.

Yrigoyen, Fajardo (Ed). Pueblos Indígenas. Constituciones y Reformas Políticas en América Latina (Indigenous peoples. Constitutions and Political Reforms in Latin America). Lima: IIDS, 2010.

Wilson, Jeffrey (2015). Understanding resource nationalism: economy dynamics and political institutions. In: *Contemporary politics.* 21(49): 399-416.

Wilson, Jeffrey (2013). *Governing Global production, resource networks in the Asia – Pacific steel industry.* Great Britain: Pallgrave Macmillan.

Zanatta, Loris (2012). *Historia de América Latina. De la colonia al siglo XXI* (History of Latin America. From Colony to the 21st century). México: Siglo XXI Press.

Biographical Sketch

Name: Nidia Catherine González Piñeros

Affiliation: Research Fellow, School of Political and Social Sciences, University of Bologna, Italy

Education:

2002/2005 PhD. Philosophy at Institute of Political Science, "Johannes Gutenberg Universität-Mainz," Germany

2000/2001 Studies in German Spanish Translation, "Universidad Nacional," Colombia

1996/2000 B.F.A. Political Science, "Universidad Nacional," Colombia

Research and Professional Experience:

Research Associate/School of Political y Social Science, University of Bologna 10.2015/04.2017

Professor/School of Political y Social Science, University of Bologna, Ravenna and Bologna, Italy 02.2014/09.2015

Undergraduate classes: - History and Institutions in Latin America

Postgraduate classes: - Contemporary History of the Relations between Europe and Latin America: society, politics, ethno-cultural rights

Associate Professor, Faculty of Economics and Social Science. University of La Salle, Bogotá, Colombia

07.2011/06.2012

Undergraduate classes:

- State/Nation Theory
- Democracy and Citizenship

Postgraduate classes:

- Research Methodology

Associate Professor, Faculty of Politic and International Relations. Sergio Arboleda University, Bogotá, Colombia

01.2010/06.2011

Undergraduate classes:

- State Theory
- Political Analysis Methodology
- Collective Action and Social Movements

Director of political institutions department

Director of the research Group "GAP"

Associate Professor, Law Faculty, Santo Tomás University, Colombia

02.2009/11.2012

Postgraduate classes:

- Research Methodology

– Social Movements and Civil Society, Ethnic Movements in the Andes

Responsible for the Undergraduate program on Government and International Business

Guest Teacher M.F.A in Latin-American Philosophy, Santo Tomás University, Bogotá.

01.2010/01.2012

Postgraduate classes:

– Social Movements and Civil Society
– Ethnic Movements in the Andes

Guest teacher, B.F.A. Political Science, Nacional University, Bogotá.

08.2008/06.2009

Undergraduate classes:

– Collective Action
– Political Analysis Methodology

Guest teacher, M.F.A in Political Science, Andes University, Bogotá.

08.2008/12.2008

Postgraduate classes:

– Quantitative Methodology for Social Scientists

Associate Professor, Faculty of Humanities, Pontificia Universidad Javeriana, Cali, Colombia

01.2006/08.2008

Undergraduate classes:

– Political Analysis Methodology
– Quantitative Methodology for Political Scientists

Postgraduate classes:

– Peace Initiatives in Colombia
– Peace-building

Director of Postgraduate Programs, Faculty of Humanities

Assistant Professor. Law Faculty, San Buenaventura University, Cali, Colombia

01.2004/05.2005

Undergraduate classes:

– Methodology for Political Scientists
– Political Philosophy

Teacher of the no formal Education Programs

Native social projects: "Proyecto Nasa," "Asociación de Cabildos Indígenas del Norte del Cauca," Colombia

08.2003/08.2008

Workshops:

- Indigenous people on the constitution of 1991
- United Nations working group for indigenous political participation
- Globalization and sustainability

Support for the publication:

"Proyecto Nasa: un sueño para continuar con las raíces en la tierra"

Founder of the Radio program "Nasa women taking part in the future of Nasa project"

Assistant Researcher, Deutsches Forschung Gesellschaft DFG Political Sciences Department, Johannes Gutenberg Universität - Mainz, Germany

07.2001/01.2003

Support for the publications:

- "Experimentelle Konfliktforschung I"
- "Experimentelle Konfliktforschung II"

Coordinator of the researchers team

Coordinator of the experiments

Recent Professional Appointments and Conferences:

July 2015 "Innovation on governance, environmental development and technological interdependence in Latin America." International Conference Sustainable Environmental Politics and Economy, Freie Universitaet Berlin.

June 2015 "Innovation on Governance, Inclusion and Sustainability: Plurinational Constitutions and Energetical Nationalism in Latin America." International Conference The 8th NOLAN Conference "Struggles over Resources in Latin America." University of Helsinki.

March 2014 "Mobilitazione e Nazione Plurinazionale: comparando i casi di Colombia e Bolivia" (Mobilization and plurinational State, Comparing the Cases of Colombia and Bolivia). Seminar "Indigenous Populations in the Contemporary World: Identity, Resistance and Rights" Università degli Studi di Bologna, Ravenna, Italy.

March 2014 "Democrazia e pluralità, da diritti etnici a costituzioni plurinazionali, 1991-2012 (Democracy and Plurality, from Ethnical Rights to plurinational Constitutions, 1991-2012). Center of Latin American Studies, Università degli Studi di Bologna, Bologna, Italy.

May 2013 "America indigena e stati nazionali: temi e problemi" (Native Americans and National States: Issues in the 21st Century). 35th International American Studies Annual Meeting. Dissgea, "Circolo Amerindiano," Università degli Studi di Padova, Italy.

April 2013 "Lo Stato Plurinazionale in Bolivia" (Plurinational State in Bolivia), Lecture of History and Institutions in Latin America, Università degli Studi di Bologna, Bologna, Italy.

May 2012 "Movilización indígena, cultura política y Estado, comparando Bolivia y Colombia" (Indigenous Mobilitisation, Political Culture and State, Comparing the Cases of Bolivia and Colombia) Permanent Seminar on methods and issues of Native American contemporary history. Università degli Studi di Padova, Padova, Italy.

Publications Last Three Years:

2014 Rivista di studi Iberoamericani, Confluenze. Vol. 6, No. 2 (2014) ISSN 2036-0967. pp. 29-38: "Democrazia e pluralità in America Latina, da diritti etnici a costituzioni plurinazionali (1991-2012)" (Democracy and Plurality, from Ethnical Rights to plurinational Constitutions).

2013 Rivista di Studi Iberoamericani, Confluenze (Journal of Studies Iberoamerican, Confluenze). Vol. 5, No. 2 (2013) ISSN 2036-0967. pp. 107-118: "Retos y Encrujadas del Estado en Bolivia, entre la naturaleza estatal y lo plurinacional" (Challenges and crossroads of the plurinational Bolivian State).

2013 In: Dallo stato del bienestar allo stato del buenvivir (The state of the state of bienestar buenvivir). "Sfide e tensioni nello Stato plurinazionale boliviano" (Challenges and Crossroads of the Plurinational Bolivian State) Bologna: Filodiritto Editore. pp. 136 155. ISBN: 978-88-95922-46-1.

2012 Revista Equidad y Desarrollo (Equity and Development Magazine), No. 17, January-June. ISSN: 1692-7311, pp. 133-148. "Estado, nación y democracia en el siglo XXI" (State, nation and democracy in the 21st century).

In: Bolivia
Editor: Glen Mendoza

ISBN: 978-1-63484-886-2

Chapter 4

CAMELID POPULATIONS AND SOIL CLASSIFICATION AND FERTILITY IN THE NORTHWEST OF LA PAZ (BOLIVIA)

M. A. Muñoz, A. Faz, R. Zornoza, S. Martínez-Martínez and J. A. Acosta
Sustainable Use, Management, and Reclamation of Soil and Water Research Group, Department of Agrarian Science and Technology, Polytechnic University of Cartagena , Cartagena, Spain

ABSTRACT

Camelid populations are located at the Andean Plateau and produce essential incomes for native human population in Bolivia. Vicuna (*Vicugna vicugna*) is a wild endangered species which share territory and resources with other domestic camelids like alpaca (*Lama pacos*) in the National Apolobamba Integrated Area. Apolobamba is one of the poorest zones in La Paz Department. However, some natural resources such as the soil are much unknown. Further information is needed to determine their capacity to sustain the grazing activity in this area. The objectives of this survey were: a) to provide their edaphological classifications, b) to characterize the soil profiles in 8 zones with different vicuna and alpaca populations and c) to study their fertility based on physico-chemical properties. The investigation was conducted in Apolobamba Area, located in the Northwest of La Paz Department. Eight zones were selected taking into account the vicuna populations and the alpaca densities based on the last censuses data. One soil profile was identified in each zone and one sample was collected from each horizon. Two different key soil taxonomies were used to classify the soils. The most relevant physico-chemical soil properties were studied to characterize the soils and to determine the fertility. Six different types of soils were identified according to the soil classifications in the 8 studied zones. In general, soils presented medium-high organic carbon, total nitrogen, total phosphorus, cation exchange capacity and exchangeable cation contents. Moreover, the soils exhibited low electrical conductivity, acid pH, null equivalent calcium carbonate contents and different textures. Regarding to the soil fertility, the zones with higher vicuna and medium and low alpaca populations exhibited better fertility according to the soil properties studied in the profiles. Conversely, higher alpaca populations and lower vicuna populations were located in those soils with lower fertility (zones 1 and 3). Based on these results, higher alpaca concentration seemed to be associated to lower soil fertility while higher vicuna populations were located in soils with better fertility (zones 7 and 8). This observation points out the necessity to carry out conservation actions in order to preserve the soil fertility particularly in zone 1. However, these actions should consider that productions from both wild and domestic camelids are one of the most important economical activities in Apolobamba.

Keywords: Bolivian Andean Plateau, camelids, soil profiles, physico-chemical properties, soil fertility

INTRODUCTION

Andean Plateau is the main mountain range of the American continent with more than 7,500 km. These high-elevation ecosystems extend from 11° N to 56° S (Arroyo and Cavieres, 2013) and involve Argentina, Chile, Bolivia, Peru, Ecuador, Colombia and Venezuela. The Northern Andes is called paramo and is characterized by humid climate while the Central and Southern Andes dryer zone is called puna. Andean Plateau ecosystems are undergoing transition to agricultural activities and cattle grazing in South America. There is a lack of information determining the contributions of these land uses to soil degradation and nutrient loss (Otero et al. 2011). According to Podwojewski and Poulenard (2000), anthropogenic factors are the main cause of these ecosystems degradation, as a consequence of physical and chemical soil alterations. Rocha and Sáez (2003) suggested Andean ecosystems degradation as a consequence of the change on soil use, unsuitable water management and the excessive cattle grazing in the Andean Plateau.

Vicuna (*Vicugna vicugna,* Molina, 1782) is one of the few large native herbivores of the South American puna (Franklin, 1983). According to the Red List Category and Criteria, it is a 'Least Concern' species from 2008 based on International Union Conservation of Nature classification (IUCN, 2015). Their fleece is one of the finest fibers in the world and it is considered a keystone resource for inhabitants of the region (Laker and Gordon, 2006). Wild and domestic camelids usually share natural resources such as soil and vegetation in the Andean habitats (Borgnia et al. 2008).

The National Apolobamba Integrated Management Area is located in the Andean Plateau of the northwest of La Paz, Bolivia, that borders with the Republic of Peru. Aymara and Quechua indigenous communities live in Apolobamba and one of the main economic activities is the camelid cattle husbandry (Agencia Española de Cooperación Internacional, 2004). The index of poverty of the municipalities in Apolobamba is around 98% based on data from census carried out in Bolivia as it is considered one of the poorest zones in Bolivia (Instituto Nacional de Estadística, 2015). Regarding to data from the last census conducted by the Servicio Nacional de Áreas Protegidas of Bolivia (SERNAP), Apolobamba hosts more than 10,000 vicunas and 130,000 alpacas (*Lama pacos*), approximately 34% of the total alpacas in Bolivia. They are distributed around 1200 km^2 in the puna at Apolobamba (SERNAP, 2006) where no agriculture activities are carried out. The vicuna programme in the puna of Apolobamba is an example of sustainable management of the biodiversity at the Andean Mountain Range (Agencia Española de Cooperación Internacional, 2004).

However, some natural resources connected with the camelid grazing such as the soil are much unknown in high altitude grasslands (Milchunas and Lauenroth, 1993; Schuman et al. 1999, Muñoz et al. 2015). Mountain soils are often poorly developed because of the high slopes, erosion and other factors (Legros, 1992; Catoni et al. 2016). Soil property determination can contribute to the understanding of the soil fertility and the grazing impact (Dorrough et al. 2006; Li et al. 2008; Muñoz et al. 2015). Therefore, further information is needed to determine their capacity for sustaining the grazing activity in this area. The objectives of this survey were: a) to provide their edaphological classifications, b) to characterize the soil profiles in 8 zones with different vicuna and alpaca populations and c) to study their fertility based on physico-chemical properties.

Materials and Methods

The survey was conducted at the puna in Apolobamba area, the habitat of wild and domestic camelids. The coordinates were 68° 30′–69° 20′W and 14° 40′–15° 10′S (SERNAP, 2006). This ecosystem was located between 4500 and 5500 m.a.s.l. (Muñoz et al. 2012). The study area is characterized by udic and frigid soil moisture and temperature regimes (USDA, 2014) with an annual average temperature of 4.5°C and 505 mm annual precipitation which is concentrated in five months, between November and March (SERNAP, 2015). The zone exhibits a mountain landscape influenced by glacial processes and parent materials such as metamorphic pelite with slate, metalimonite and sandstone (SERNAP, 2006). The most plentiful plant community is *Pycnophyllum* grassland with the variant *Selaginella* (Seibert, 1993; Muñoz et al. 2015).

Studied Zones

Because of the importance of the vicuna management programme for inhabitants of the puna in Apolobamba, the density of vicuna populations was the main criterion to select the zones where edaphological classification and soil characterization were determined. According to Borgnia et al. (2010) vicuna populations usually inhabited in the same zones limited by natural geographical barriers. They presented a territorial and sedentary behavior that triggered a stable population in a particular zone. Based on these findings and data from the different censuses, vicuna populations were located in determined areas in Apolobamba. Eight zones with stable populations were selected based on data from the last vicuna censuses conducted in Apolobamba from 2000 to 2005 (SERNAP, 2006). The location of the studied zones and the Apolobamba area is shown in Figure 1.

The selected zones presented similar vicuna densities in pairs: 1–2 low vicuna density (2.1-9.4 individual km^{-2}), 3–4 medium vicuna density (9.4-16.5 individual km^{-2}), 5–6 high vicuna density (16.5-23.1 individual km^{-2}) and 7–8 very high vicuna density (23.1-58.1 individual km^{-2}). Alpaca density was also taken into account regarding the last census conducted in the area (SERNAP, 2006). Zones 2, 4, 5, 6, 7 and 8 hosted 57.0-112.0 individual km^{-2} while zone 1 and zone 3 hosted 113.0-171.0 and 172.0-331.0 individual km^{-2}, respectively.

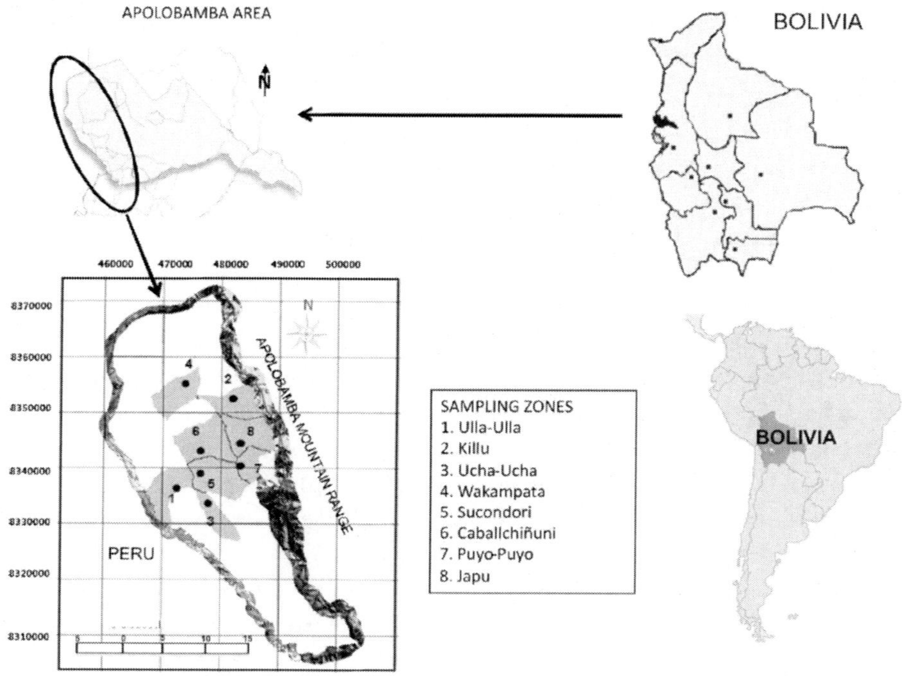

Figure 1. Studied zone location.

Physico-Chemical Properties

In order to classify and characterize the soil, a representative soil profile was opened and all the morphological horizons were identified. One sample was collected per horizon. Soil profiles were classified using USDA (2014) and World Reference Base for Soil Resources (IUSS Working Group WRB, 2015) systems. Samples were placed in plastics bags, then sealed and transported to the laboratory. Soil samples were air-dried and passed through a 2 mm sieve to remove gravels, plant remains and root fragments.

The following physico-chemical properties were determined: total organic carbon (TOC) was determined using a TOC Analyzer (Shimadzu 5000, Japan); total nitrogen (TN) was measured according to the Kjeldahl method (Duchaufour, 1970); available phosphorous was determined using the method of Watanabe and Olsen (1965); cation exchange capacity (CEC) and exchangeable cations according to Chapman (1965); pH was measured in 1:1

(w/v) aqueous solution (Peech, 1965) and texture through the pipette Robinson method and the texture classes were established following FAO (2006).

Results and Discussion

Edaphological Classification

Five horizons were identified in zones 1, 2 and 4. Four horizons were observed in zones 5 and 8 while three horizons were determined in zones 3, 6 and 7. Since A horizons were identified on soil profiles, anthropical influence could be inferred due to the camelid grazing in the studied area. Two A horizons were observed in zones 4 and 8 whereas zone 2 exhibited three A horizons. The diagnostic horizon Bw was identified in the whole of profiles except of zone 1. Four different C horizons were identified in zone 1 whereas one Cg horizon was observed in zone 4.

According to USDA (2014) classification, soils in zones 5, 6 and 4 were classified as Typic Dystrudept whereas zone 2 was Humic Dystrudept. Zone 1 was Typic Udipsamment while zone 3 was Oxyaquic Udipsamment. Zones 7 and 8 were Entic Hapludoll and Typic Udorthent, respectively. Based on the WRB soil classification system (ISSS Working Group WRB, 2015), the main groups were Regosol and Cambisol. Zones 5 and 6 were classified as Haplic Cambisol whereas zone 4 was Endogleyic Cambisol. Zone 1 was Arenic Regosol, zone 3 was Regosol and zone 8 was Haplic Regosol. Zone 2 was classified as Cambic Umbrisol and zone 7 as Haplic Phaeozem.

Physico-Chemical Soil Characterization

Physico-chemical results are shown in Table 1. Based on results found by Muñoz and Faz (2012), soils presented medium-high organic carbon in comparison with other highlands located in mountain ranges (Gentxu et al. 2008; Wu et al. 2003). Comparatively, zone 1 exhibited a very low TOC content. The highest surface TOC contents were observed in zones 4, 7 and 8.

Table 1. Physico-chemical parameters analyzed in the studied zones

Horizon	Depth	TOC	TN	P_2O_5	CEC	pH	EC	Clay	Silt
	(cm)	(g kg^{-1})	(g kg^{-1})	(mg kg^{-1})	($cmol_+$ kg^{-1})		(µS cm^{-1})	(%)	
Zone 1									
A	0-10	6.3	0.8	51.9	9.3	4.5	190.0	7.0	16.9
C1	10-36	2.8	0.6	16.8	6.1	5.0	271.0	8.9	17.1
C2	36-60	1.7	0.3	15.0	5.4	4.9	144.0	9.8	10.6
C3	60-80	2.1	0.5	49.6	6.0	4.9	307.0	12.5	13.0
C4	>80	2.2	0.5	31.2	5.7	4.9	433.0	11.6	8.7
Zone 2									
A1	0-5	46.8	4.5	148.2	17.2	5.6	53.5	20.2	33.8
A2	5-10	34.5	3.7	110.6	12.5	5.7	39.3	18.8	33.0
A3	10-20	18.4	2.0	16.8	10.9	6.2	29.2	17.3	35.8
Bw	20-36	11.4	1.5	27.6	10.0	6.1	25.2	16.1	32.1
C	>36	11.5	1.5	26.5	10.1	6.7	23.9	16.9	32.7
Zone 3									
A	0-10	41.7	3.3	81.4	12.2	5.6	414.0	5.9	10.0
C1	10-26	11.7	1.2	47.0	5.7	5.6	296.0	7.8	12.8
C2	>26	2.7	0.5	21.2	5.0	6.0	167.0	9.3	14.2
Zone 4									
A1	0-9	144.7	8.7	254.9	29.2	4.9	290.0	25.3	44.1
A2	9-23	55.3	5.1	223.9	25.2	5.6	38.7	18.4	44.0
Bw	23-50	18.9	2.2	183.1	10.3	5.5	35.6	24.1	55.0
Cg	50-62	4.6	0.7	135.3	5.8	5.3	39.6	17.1	61.2
Cg/R	>62	4.4	0.7	65.1	1.1	6.1	26.7	12.4	38.7
Zone 5									
A	0-9	50.4	4.5	167.2	18.6	5.9	78.1	30.4	37.9
Bw	9-29	28.4	3.6	156.8	12.7	6.6	61.3	39.8	44.7
C1	29-47	10.8	1.4	81.7	6.8	7.1	29.2	33.6	44.5
C2	>47	5.5	0.5	77.3	2.7	7.2	29.6	20.6	31.2
Zone 6									
A	0-18	47.9	3.4	166.9	17.4	4.2	92.7	12.5	31.8
Bw	18-33	15.8	1.6	145.8	8.5	4.2	55.0	14.5	39.9
C	>33	4.8	0.6	138.4	6.0	4.8	33.0	12.6	22.2
Zone 7									
A	0-18	90.0	6.5	123.6	17.3	5.2	487.0	12.1	38.0
Bw	18-33	23.4	1.9	37.0	8.6	5.9	56.7	9.6	33.5
C	>33	4.2	0.7	2.0	8.2	6.1	32.4	14.0	36.3
Zone 8									
A1	0-7	73.0	5.9	94.3	19.7	3.9	97.6	16.6	55.5
A2	7-12	45.3	3.5	80.2	16.8	4.2	80.7	15.8	46.4
Bw	12-24	26.0	2.3	86.3	10.5	4.5	33.2	12.5	28.6
C	>24	18.2	1.7	67.9	7.3	4.4	17.1	9.4	24.7

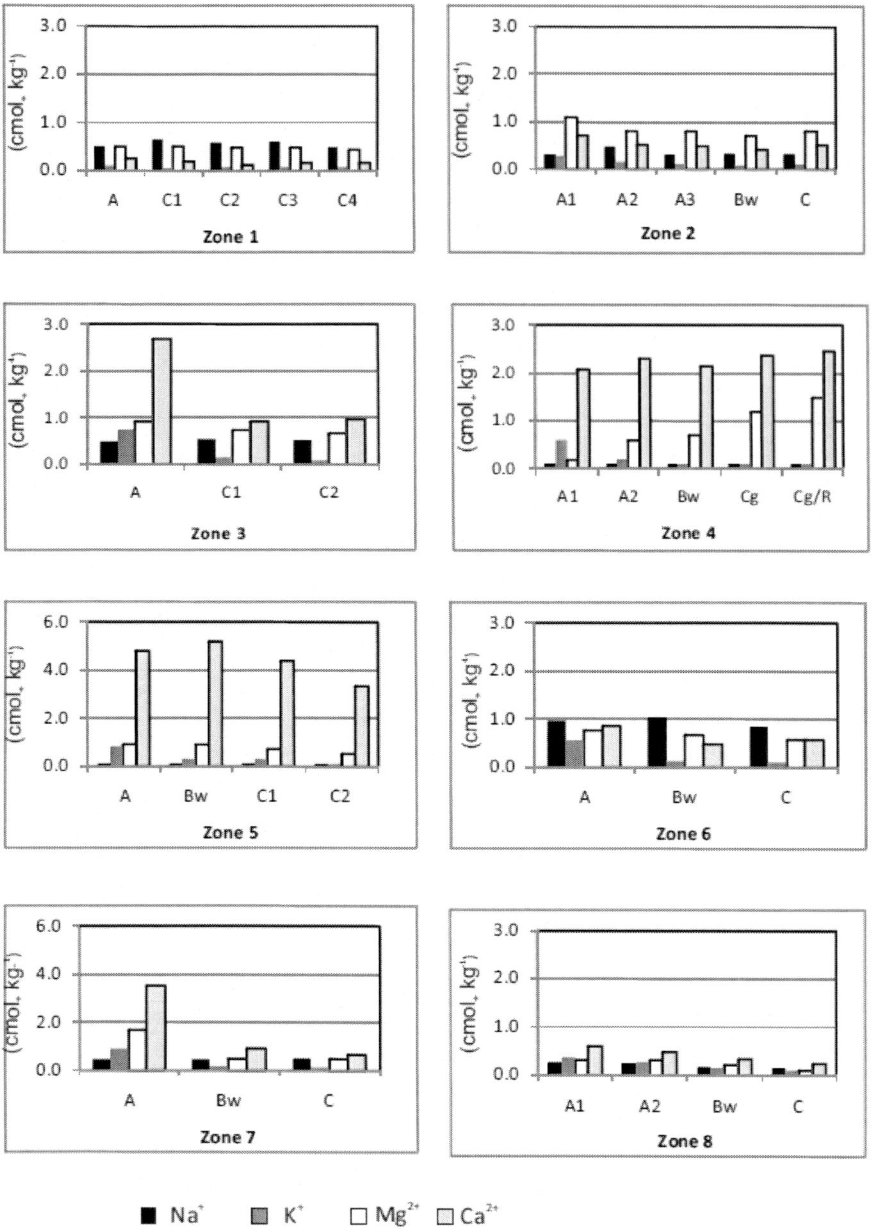

Figure 2. Exchangeable cations (Na^+, K^+, Mg^{2+} and Ca^{2+}) per horizon in the studied zones.

Total nitrogen, P_2O_5 and CEC presented the same trend. These parameters generally decreased in depth. Taking into account the balance of nutrients required for microorganisms (Brady and Weil, 2008), all studied zones showed C/N values within the optimum average in the surface horizon, around 12, with the exception of zone 1 (7.9) and zone 4 (16.6) where humification processes could be more intense than SOM mineralization in this zone. Cation exchange capacity values in the surface horizons were generally high (Urbano, 2011) except for zones 1 and 3. According to the survey conducted by Wilcox et al. (1988) in the Peruvian puna, it could be attributed to high quantities of organic matter or/and poorly crystalline clays derived from volcanic ash.

The highest exchangeable K^+ and Mg^{2+} contents were observed in zone 7 while the lowest ones were observed in zone 1 and 4, respectively (Figure 2). The highest Na^+ content was found in zone 6 and the lowest one in zone 5. Regarding to the Ca^{2+} contents, the highest concentration was observed in zone 5 and the lowest in zone 1.

Zone 8 was extremely acid (Table 1), while the other zones were very strongly acid and strongly acid (Soil Survey Division Staff, 1993). Studied soils exhibited low electrical conductivity (Soil Survey Division Staff, 1993) and null equivalent calcium carbonate contents (data not shown). Texture analyses showed sandy-loam and loam soils (FAO, 2006) with the lowest clay contents in zones 3 and 1 (Table 1).

Camelid Densities and Soil Fertility

With respect to the TN contents and CEC, in general all the studied zones showed concentrations above the mean value established by Vagen et al. (2006) in grasslands at highlands for good fertility (3.90 g kg^{-1}), as the same for CEC (11.76 $cmol_{(+)}$ kg^{-1}) except for zone 1. Moreover, C/N and exchangeable cation contents supported this finding in zone 1. In general, the studied zones presented a good fertility based on clay contents and Vagel et al. (2006) classification. However, zones 3 and 1 were very distant to the minimum content of clay contents.

The zones with higher vicuna and medium and low alpaca populations exhibited better fertility according to the soil properties studied in the profiles as results from zones 7 and 8 showed. Additionally, zone 4 (medium vicuna and low alpaca populations) exhibited high TOC contents and high C/N ratio. Conversely, higher alpaca populations were located in zones with low CEC and clay contents, identified in zones 1 and 3. These zones presented low and medium vicuna populations. Based on these results, higher alpaca concentration seemed to be associated to lower soil fertility while higher vicuna populations were located in soils with higher fertility. Moreover, zone 1 presented the lowest soil fertility regarding the physico-chemical soil properties studied. Disturbed vegetation was observed in zones 1 and 2 supporting camelid grazing affection (Muñoz and Faz, 2012; Muñoz et al. 2015).

Conclusion

Anthropical influence could be inferred due to the camelid grazing in the 8 studied zones. six different types of soils were identified following to the two soil classifications. The groups Dystrudept, Regosol and Cambisol were the most abundant. The soil characterization showed the highest TOC, TN, P_2O_5 and CEC in zones 4, 7 and 8 while the highest exchangeable cation contents were identified in zones 5, 6 and 7. In general, zone 1 exhibited the lowest values of the physico-chemical properties studied. Higher vicuna and medium and low alpaca populations were identified in zones with better fertility. Conversely, higher alpaca concentration seemed to be associated to lower soil fertility while although further studies should be conducted in order to clarify it. This suggestion points out the necessity to carry out conservation actions particularly in zone 1, in order to preserve its soil fertility. However, these actions should consider that productions from both wild and domestic camelids are one of the most important economical activities in Apolobamba.

Acknowledgments

We thank the Agencia Española de Cooperación Internacional para el Desarrollo (AECID) and the Herbario Nacional de Bolivia for their cooperation and support.

REFERENCES

Agencia Española de Cooperación Internacional (2004). *Manejo Sostenible de la Vicuña en Apolobamba* (Sustainable Management in Apolobamba Vicuña). In: Mudarra, F., Muñoz, M.A. *Agencia Española de Cooperación Internacional- Programa Araucaria* (Eds). La Paz. 149 pp.

Arroyo, M., Cavieres, L. (2013). High Elevation Andean Ecosystems. In: Simon, A. (editor). *Encyclopedia of Biodiversity* (Second Editon), pp 96-110.

Borgnia, M., Vilá, B. L., Cassini, M. H. (2008). Interaction between wild camelids and livestock in an Andean semi-desert. *J Arid Environ.,* 72, 2150-2158.

Borgnia, M., Vilá, B. L., Cassini, M. H. (2010). Foraging ecology of Vicuna, *Vicugna vicugna*, in dry puna of Argentina. *Small Ruminant Res.* 88, 44-53.

Brady, N., Weil, R. (2008). *The Nature and Properties of Soil.* Pearson International Edition, New Jersey. 975 pp.

Catoni, M., D`Amico, M., Zanini, E., Bonifacio, E. (2016). Effect of pedogenic processes and formation factors on organic matter stabilization in alpine forest soils. *Geoderma,* 263, 151-160.

Chapman, H. D. (1965). Cation exchange capacity. In: Black, C.A. (Ed.), *Methods of Soil analysis.* American Society of Agronomy, Madison, Wisconsin, pp. 891-900.

Dorrough, J., Moxham, C., Turner, V., Sutter, G. (2006). Soil phosphorus and tree cover modify the effects of livestock grazing on plant species richness in Australian grassy woodland. *Biol. Conserv.,* 130 (3), 394-405.

Duchaufour, P. (1970). Precis de Pedologie. Masson, Paris. 482 pp.

FAO (2006). Guidelines for soil description, *Food and Agriculture Organization of the United Nations*, 4th Edition, Rome. 97 pp.

Genxu, W., Yuanshou, L., Yibo, W., Qingbo, W. (2008). Effects of permafrost thawing on vegetation and soil carbon pool losses on the Qinghai-Tibet Plateau, China. *Geoderma* 143 (1-2), 143-152.

Instituto Nacional de Estadística (2015). Available from URL: http://www.ine.gov.bo/indice/Estadisticasocial.aspx.

IUCN, 2015. The IUCN Red list of Threatened species. International Union for Conservation of Nature. Available from URL: http://www.iucnredlist.org/details/22956/0.

IUSS Working Group WRB (2015). World Reference Base for Soil Resources 2014, update 2015 International soil classification system for naming soils and creating legends for soil maps. World Soil Resources Reports No. 106. FAO, Rome. 192 pp.

Laker, J., Gordon I. (2006). Desafíos para el uso sostenible de la vicuña y el rol del Proyecto Manejo de camélidos Sudamericanos Silvestres (MACS). (Challenges for sustainable use of vicuña and the role of the Wild South American Camelids Management Project). In: Vilá, B (Ed.). *Investigación, Conservación y Manejo de vicuñas*. Luján, pp 9-15.

Legros, J. P. 1992. Soils of Alpine Mountains. I. P. Martini, W. Chesworth (Eds.), *Weathering, Soils Andpaleosols,* Elsevier, Amsterdam, Netherlands, pp. 155–181.

Li, Ch., Hao, X., Zhao, M., Han, G., Willms, W. D. (2008). Influence of historic sheep grazing on vegetation and soil properties of a Desert Steppe in Inner Mongolia. *Agric. Ecosyst. Environ.* 128 (1-2), 109-116.

Milchunas, D. G., Lauenroth, W. K. (1993). Quantitative effects of grazing on vegetation and soils over a global range of environments. *Ecol Monogr.,* 63, 327-366.

Muñoz, M. A., Faz, A. (2012). Soil organic matter stocks and quality at high altitude grasslands of Apolobamba, Bolivia. *Catena* 94, 26-35.

Muñoz, M. A., Faz, A., Acosta J. A., Martínez-Martínez, S., Zornoza, R. (2015). Effect of South American grazing camelids on soil fertility and vegetation at the Bolivian Andean grasslands. *Agriculture, Ecosystems and Environment* 207, 203-210.

Otero, J. D., Figueroa, A., Muñoz, F. A., Peña, M. R. (2011). Loss of soil and nutrients by surface runoff in two agro-ecosystems within an Andean paramo area. *Ecol. Eng*. 37, 2035– 2043.

Peech, M. (1965). Hidrogen-ion activity. In: Black, C. A. (Ed.), *Methods of Soil Analysis*. American Society of Agronomy, Madison, Wisconsin, pp. 914-916.

Podwojewski, P., Poulenard, J. (2000). La degradación de los suelos de los páramos: Los Suelos del Páramo (The degradation of the moors: Soils of Páramo). In: Mena, P. A. Josse, C., Medina, G. (eds.). Serie Páramo. Los suelos del páramo 5 (Paramo series. Moorland soils 5). GTP/Abya Yala, Quito, pp 27-36.

Rocha, O., Sáez, C. (2003). Uso pastoril en humedales altoandinos (Pastoral use in high Andean wetlands). In: Rocha, O., Sáez, C., and Ministerio de Desarrollo Sostenible y Planificación (Eds.), La Paz. 195 pp.

Schuman, G. E., Reeder, J. D., Manely, J. T., Hart, R. H., Manely, W. A. (1999). Impact of grazing management on the carbon and nitrogen balance of a mixed-grass rangeland. *Ecol Appl.,* 9, 65–71.

Seibert, P. (1993). *Ecología en Bolivia* (Ecology in Bolivia). Instituto de Ecología-Universidad Mayor de San Andrés, Revista de Ecología N 20. 84 pp.

SERNAP (2015). Área Natural de Manejo Integrado Nacional Apolobamba, Características del Área (Natural Integrated Management Area National Apolobamba area Features). Available from URL: <http://www.sernap.gob.bo/images/descargas/areas.pdf>.

SERNAP (2006). Plan de Manejo, *Área Natural de Manejo Integrado Nacional Apolobamba* (Natural Area Apolobamba National Integrated Management), La Paz, Unpublished results. 35 pp.

Soil Survey Division Staff (1993). *Soil survey manual.* USDA Handbook 18. U.S. Government Printing Office, Washington, DC.

Urbano, P. (2001). *Tratado de Fitotecnia General* (Treaty of Plant General). Second Edition. Mundi-Prensa, Madrid. 501 pp.

USDA (2014). *Keys to Soil Taxonomy,* 12th Edition USDA-Natural Resources Conservation Service, Washington, DC. 360 pp.

Vagen, T. G., Shepherd, K. D., Walsh, M. G., 2006. Sensing landscape level change in soil fertility following deforestation and conversion in the highlands of Madagascar using Vis-NIR spectroscopy. *Geoderma* 133, 281–294.

Watanabe, F. S., Olsen, S. R. (1965). Test of ascorbic acid method for determining phosphorous in water and NaHCO3 extracts from soil. *Soil Sci. Soc. Am. Proc.* 677-678.

Wilcox, B. P., Allen, B. L., Bryant, F. C. (1988). Description and classification of soils of the high-elevation grasslands of central Peru. *Geoderma* 42 (1), 79-94.

Wu, H., Guo, Z., Peng, C. (2003). Land use induced changes of organic carbon storage in soils of China. *Global Change Biology* 9, 305-315.

In: Bolivia
Editor: Glen Mendoza

ISBN: 978-1-63484-886-2

Chapter 5

EFFECT OF ARTESANAL GOLD MINE ACTIVITIES ON METALS AND METALLOIDS CONTENTS IN SOILS AND SEDIMENTS FROM APOLOBAMBA, BOLIVIA

J. A. Acosta*[*], *A. Faz, M. A. Muñoz, R. Zornoza and S. Martínez-Martínez
Sustainable Use, Management,
and Reclamation of Soil and Water Research Group,
Technical University of Cartagena, Cartagena, Spain

ABSTRACT

Artisanal and small-scale gold mining activities in Apolobamba area, northwest of La Paz, Bolivia, may produce serious environmental concern and great risk to human health. The current methods used to extract gold through the amalgamation process result in metal contamination of soil and water, as well as a negative effect on health of miners and inhabitants. Two main sources of contamination has been identified, the large amount of Hg used for gold extraction and the arsenic in the arsenopyrite from gold ores; also other metals, such as Zn, Pb, Cu and Cd, are associated to mining operations and may contribute to environmental pollution. The objectives of this work were to characterize

[*] Email: ja.acosta@upct.es.

the contamination of Hg, As, Cu, Cd, Pb and Zn in soils and sediments, and to assess the risk to human health and environment in different cooperatives mines in the highlands of Bolivia. In order to achieve these objectives, soils and sediments samples were collected, and physical-chemical properties and Hg, As, Pb, Cu, Zn and Cd analysed. Results showed that As and Hg concentrations were higher in top soils than in subsurface soils in the Sunchulli-Viscachani area, indicating active As/Hg atmospheric deposition, whose concentrations exceeded the soil Hg and As threshold levels. Oppositelly, concentrations of Cd and Zn largely exceed the thresholds levels in Katantika and Sural mining districts. These data indicated that a potential risk for human and environment could be taking place. In addition, Sunchullí and Viscachani lake sediments were contaminated by Hg, As, Cd, Zn and Cu, while Katantica lake showed high concentrations of Zn, Cd and Hg, and in the Sural lake were reported high levels of As, Zn and Cu. Results showed that Cu, Pb, As and Hg concentrations in sediments from the Sunchulli River; As, Hg and Cu in the Pelechuco River, and As and Hg in the Rayo Rojo River come from mine direct discharges into the rivers. These concentrations may cause a serious problem for aquatic life, related ecosystems and human health. Therefore, there is a need to study metals and metalloids availability and speciation in soils and sediments to better understand the cycling of these elements and transfer of metals/metalloids from soils into the food chain in the area.

Keywords: metals, metalloids, gold mine, Bolivia

INTRODUCTION

The mining industry, particularly Au and Zn extractions, has always been one of the pillars of the national economy in Bolivia (Loayza and Franco 2000). The "Apolobamba Integrated Management National Area (ANMINA)" located in the northwest part of the Department of La Paz, Bolivia, is a very important gold mining region. Currently gold is extracted using an Hg amalgamation technique that represents a highly economical and practical technique since 1556 (Enríquez 2001). Hg amalgamation is based on the formation of gold-Hg alloy which is subsequently heated to volatilise Hg to obtain pure gold. However, depending upon the mining company, Hg is not recovered and 5-45% of the total Hg used can be released into the environment: soil, water and atmosphere (Malm et al. 1990; Maurice - Bourgoin et al. 1999). In addition, arsenopyrite (FeAsS) minerals that commonly occur with the Au ore deposits are likely sources of high soil As.

Therefore pollution of soils, water, and air surrounding mine areas poses threats to ecosystem and human health (Faz et al. 2003). Also, oxidation of sulfide-containing ores and mine waste produces sulfuric acid that generates acid mine drainage and increases solubility of potentially toxic elements such as As, Sb, Zn, and Cd.

The studied area has around 100 mining cooperatives and they are all located in alluvial plains in the Andean Bolivian Plateau. The National Secretary of the Environment (SENMA) carried out an evaluation of the mining and industrial sectors in Bolivia and concluded that the main impacts on the environment from the mine activity are: consumption of exhaustible and scarce resources (land use, removal of minerals, and water use); transformation of the landscape; pollution of surface water, groundwater and soil solution; accumulation of solid waste and emissions of dust containing heavy metals that can contaminate water and soils (Enríquez 2001). Recent exploratory studies also found significant Hg contamination in sediments and river waters (Maurice-Bourgoin et al. 2001), and fish (Alanoca et al. 2000).

Hg is among the most highly toxic trace metals in the food chain, and many national and international agencies and organizations are interested in developing methods for its possible emission control (Horvat et al. 2003). Hg transfer and transport in watersheds are well understood (USEPA, 2000). The elemental Hg (Hg^0) can transport from its source to the final receptor following a multi-step frequencies, which includes emission to the atmosphere, transportation and deposition. Travnikov (2005), studied the dispersion of Hg in the atmosphere of the Northern Hemisphere, and suggested that the contribution of external anthropogenic and natural sources to Hg deposition to different continents varies from 30% to 70% of the total value.

In general, Hg is believed to be relatively inert with a strong volatility under most atmospheric conditions (Zang-Ho et al. 2005). Thus, Hg^o is not easily oxidized to less volatile forms by the major oxidants (O_3, OH, etc.); so its residence time is estimated in the range of 1–2 years (Lindquist and Rhode 1985).

Arsenic in Bolivia is present mostly in the west Andean region, specifically in the zone known as "As–Ag–Pb–Zn–Cu–Au belt" (Litter and Morgada 2010), where high levels of natural contamination by arsenic is found as a result of an intense magmatic activity since the Miocene (MDSMA 1996). Elevated levels of the soil As pose environmental health risks. Inorganic As is toxic and can cause cancer in skin, lungs, urinary tracts, cardiovascular disease, neurotoxicity and diabetes (Choong et al. 2007; Guan et al. 2012; WHO, 2014).

The aims of this work were to characterize the contamination of Hg, As, Cu, Cd, Pb and Zn in soils and sediments, and to assess the risk to human health and environment in different cooperatives mines in the highlands of Bolivia.

METHODS

Study Area and Sampling

The study area is located in the protected area of "Apolobamba," 68° 30´-69° 20´ west and 14° 40´-15° 10´south, La Paz Province, Bolivia. Three different gold mining districts affected by metals and metaloids pollution (Campo, 2003) were selected for our study: Sunchullí-Viscachani, Katantica, and Sural mining areas (Figure 1).

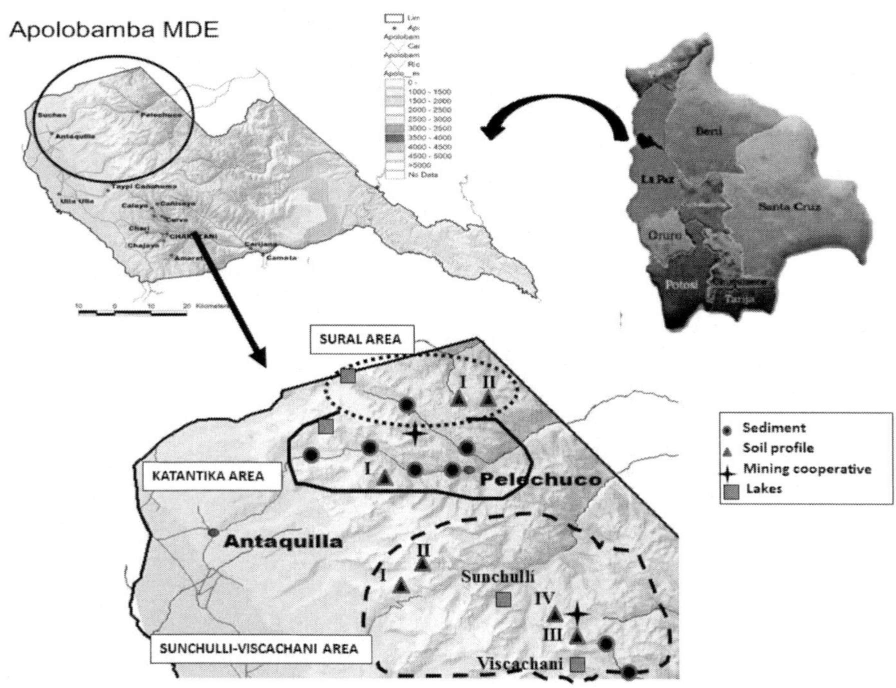

Figure 1. Sampling map and location of the three studied areas.

Four soil profiles were collected in the Sunchullí-Viscachani area. Soil profiles were classified according to the world reference base (WRB 2006). These are a Fibric Histosol (Profile I), a Haplic Cambisol (Profile II), and two Haplic Regosols (Eutric) (Profile III and IV) (Table 1). Profile I, composed by three horizons: H1 (0-12 cm), H2 (12-24 cm) and R (>24 cm), and Profile II, composed by four horizons; H1 (0-9 cm), Ah (9-24 cm), Bw (24-40 cm) and C/R (>40 cm), are located 6 km North-west of Sunchulli Lake and 18 km from the main mining operations, in the North face side of the mountain range (Figure 1). These profiles were sampled to find out whether there is a long distance atmospheric deposition by metals and metaloids in the area. Profiles III, composed by four horizons; H1 (0-11 cm), AC (11-22 cm), Bw (22-40 cm) and R (>40 cm), and IV, composed by four horizons; Ah (0-12 cm), C1 (12-32 cm), 2C2 (32-54 cm) and 2C3 (>54 cm), were located less than 500 m to the main mining operation. In order to evaluate the accumulation of metals and metaloids on the water bodies bed, seven sediment samples were taken: three in the Sunchullí Lake, two in the Viscachani Lake, and four in the Sunchullí River, two before and two after of a point of discharge.

The Katantica area is located in the north part of the Apolobamba gold mine area, close to the Sural area and includes three different rivers, Pelechuco river, being the biggest one, Turcos and Rayo Rojo rivers. The mining activity in this area, like in the others areas, is principally associated with gold extraction, but in this case the extraction is carried out from two different material: auriferous grey quartz and alluvial deposit coming from upstream and located at the bottom of the rivers. In the Katantika area, one soil profile (Profile I), composed by two horizons: Ah (0-42 cm) and C (> 42 cm) and located 1 km from the mining operation was examined and classified as a Lithic Leptosol (WRB, 2006). Two sediment samples in the Katantika Lake, two in the Pelechuco river (one samples before and one after the points of discharge), one in Rayo Rojo river and one in Turcos river were collected.

The smallest gold mining area included in this study, the Sural area, is located in the Northwest part of Apolobamba. In this region the principal gold extraction is from alluvial deposit in the lower part of the river, and the gold distribution is controlled by the sediment structure affected by surface runoff. Profiles I composed by two horizons: Ah (0-42 cm) and C (> 42 cm) and profile II, composed by two horizons: Ah (0-42 cm) and C (> 42 cm) were taken 5 km south-east from the Sural lake and 1 km east from Sural river, and classified as Lithic Leptosol and Fibric Histosol respectively (WRB, 2006). Two sediments samples in the Sural Lake were collected.

Soil samples were taken using a soil spade, with the caution of avoids of contamination between samples, cleaning the spade before use for each sample. Sediment samples were taken using a long spade, in order to take the samples separated from the river or lake shore and as closer as possible to the center of the river bed, and as far as possible from the shore of the lake. The soil and sediment samples were stored in polyethylene bags. All the samples were kept at 4°C prior to sample preparation and analyses.

Analytical Methods

Soil samples were dried to 30 ºC for 24 h, passed through a 2 mm sieve, and ground with mechanical agate mortar (Retsch RM 100) for 10-15 min before analyses. Sediment samples was dried and ground but not sieved because were composed of particles less that 2 mm.

Soils and sediments were characterized for: pH (Peech 1965), organic carbon (Anne 1945, Duchafour 1970), total nitrogen (Duchafour 1970), electrical conductivity (Bower and Wilcox 1965), particle size distribution (FAO-ISRIC, 2006), and cation exchange capacity (Chapman 1965).

An Advanced Hg Analyser (AMA-254, LECO company) was used with a detection limit of 0.5 ppb on weight basis, this equipment use solid samples, so it is not necessary any digestion of the samples. Reagent blanks and reference materials were used as the quality control samples during the analysis. Certified reference materials (CRM) were used to determine the accuracy and precision of the measurements and validate the applied methods.

Total Pb, Cu, As, Zn, and Cd were analyzed after nitric–perchloric acid digestion using the method suggested by Risser and Baker (1990). Measurements of metals were carried out using atomic absorption spectrophotometer (UNICAM SOLAAR 969/989 model). Reference soils (SO-3 and SO-4) from the Canadian Certified Reference Materials Project were used as the quality control samples during the analyses.

In order to compare the results, Belgium reference levels for Cd (0.8 mg kg^{-1}), Cu (17 mg kg^{-1}), Pb (40 mg kg^{-1}) and Zn (62 mg kg^{-1}) are considered (BWRHABTGG, 1995), while in the case of Hg and As it is considered the Holland reference values (0.3 mg Hg kg^{-1}, and 19 mg As kg^{-1}) (NMHPPE, 1994).

RESULTS AND DISCUSSION

Physical and Chemical Properties of Soil and Sediments

Results of Soil physical and chemical properties of each horizon from Sunchulli-Viscachani, Katantika and Sural areas are given in Table 1.

Table 1. Soil properties in each horizon from Sunchulli-Viscachani, Katantika and Sural areas

Soil profiles	pH	E. C. (dS m^{-1})	T.O.C. (g kg^{-1})	C.E.C. ($cmol_+ kg^{-1}$)	T. N. (g kg^{-1})	Clay (g kg^{-1})
Sunchulli-Viscachani area						
Profile I - H1 (0-12 cm)	5.55	0.20	96.6	30.57	7.7	176.8
Profile I - H2 (12-24 cm)	5.77	0.21	45.4	11.90	3.4	112.0
Profile II – H (0-9 cm)	6.91	0.25	66.2	15.26	3.8	169.3
Profile II – Ah (9-24 cm)	5.41	0.06	27.6	9.80	2.6	146.5
Profile II – Bw (24-40 cm)	6.61	0.05	16.8	7.43	1.5	81.5
Profile II - C/R (>40 cm)	5.44	0.19	19.2	5.76	1.4	89.7
Profile III – Ah (0-11 cm)	5.13	0.16	39.2	12.36	3.4	156.0
Profile III - A/C (11-22 cm)	5.27	0.12	27.0	11.01	2.1	127.3
Profile III – C (22-40 cm)	5.88	0.06	5.8	3.63	0.5	79.6
Profile IV – Ah (0-12 cm)	5.09	0.73	41.0	14.41	5.9	208.5
Profile IV – C1 (12-32 cm)	4.55	0.51	30.1	15.78	3.6	259.5
Profile IV – 2C2 (32-54cm)	5.31	0.17	20.8	12.28	1.6	161.9
Profile IV – 2C3 (>54 cm)	5.12	0.32	16.3	11.64	1.5	125.1
Katantika area						
Profile I - Ah	4.75	0.15	75.2	24.68	4.3	109.2
Profile I - C	6.40	0.04	06.6	4.14	0.5	55.0
Sural area						
Profile I - A	5.09	0.37	43.7	15.21	4.6	95.7
Profile II - H	4.04	0.11	59.8	61.01	17.0	150.8

E.C.: Electrical conductivity; T.O.C.: total organic carbon; T.N.: total nitrogen; C.E.C.: cation exchange capacity.

pH ranged from 4.55 to 6.91 in the Sunchulli-Viscachani, from 4.75 to 6.40 in Katantica and from 4.04 to 5.09 in the Sural smining districts, no carbonates were present in any soil profile. Therefore, soils in the three mining districts from strongly acid to neutral (Soil Survey Staff 2006); these low pH values promote metal solubilisation, and increased metal mobility (Kabata-Pendias and Pendias 2010). EC ranged from 0.05 to 0.73 dSm^{-1} in the Sunchulli-Viscachani, from 0.04 to 0.15 dSm^{-1} in the Katantica and from 0.11

to 0.37 dSm^{-1} in the Sural mining districts, with the highest value reported in topsoil of profile II from Sunchulli-Viscachani area (Table 1), and hence soils are non-saline (USDA 2003). TOC, TN and CEC followed the same pattern, with the highest values in the topsoil of the profiles from the three mining districts, and they are high compared with data reported by other authors in altitudinal grasslands (Zemmrich et al. 2010, Podwojewski et al. 2011); this could be related to the high vegetation cover of these areas. However, the decreased TOC and TN in the zone located near the mining operation site (profile III and IV) could give rise to the extinction of the plant cover affecting the soil stability and promoting soil erosion processes.

Table 2. Properties of the sediments from Sunchulli, Viscachani, Katantika and Sural lagoons

Lagoon sediments	pH	E. C. ($dS\ m^{-1}$)	T.O.C. ($g\ kg^{-1}$)	C.E.C. ($cmol_+\ kg^{-1}$)	T. N. ($g\ kg^{-1}$)	Clay ($g\ kg^{-1}$)
Sunchullí lagoon						
Sediment (1)	7.19	0.41	10.6	1.18	0.5	12.9
Sediment (2)	6.31	0.11	18.3	7.17	2.7	99.4
Sediment (3)	7.02	0.21	11.9	3.29	1.2	76.8
Viscachani lagoon						
Sediment (1)	5.74	0.56	218.3	34.74	16.7	205.1
Sediment (2)	5.77	0.04	89.5	42.56	9.0	277.2
Sural lagoon						
Sediment (1)	6.94	0.17	11.8	5.56	1.0	127.1
Sediment (2)	6.18	0.14	62.9	11.42	4.4	104.9
Katantika lagoon						
Sediment (1)	6.48	0.32	16.7	4.56	1.7	68.2
Sediment (2)	5.18	0.67	87.6	31.35	8.1	138.7

E.C.: Electrical conductivity; T.O.C.: total organic carbon; T.N.: total nitrogen; C.E.C.: cation exchange capacity.

Properties in the sediments of Sunchulli, Viscachani, Katantika and Sural lakes are showed in Table 2. pH values in the lakes were neutral (6.3-7.1) in Sunchulli, moderate acid (5.7) in Viscachani, sliglty acid (6.1-6.9) in Sural and from strong acid to neutral (5.18-6.49) in Katantica (Soils Survey Division Staff, 1993); what means that most of these sediments are depleted in bases, and it is is also corroborated by the absence of calcium carbonate (Cobertera, 1993). These sediments were not saline (Soils Survey Division Staff, 1993). TOC and TN concentrations of the sediments from Viscachani were the highest while in Sunchilli lagoon were the lowest, what could be explained due to the vegetation contribution. CEC showed high values in Viscachani lake, what can be related to the TOC higher concentrations, and the clay content and its composition by mainly vermiculites (Honorato, 2000).

Table 3. Properties of the sediments from Sunchulli, Pelechuco, Turcos and Rayo Rojo rivers

River sediments	pH	E. C. (dS m^{-1})	T.O.C. (g kg^{-1})	C.E.C. ($cmol_{+}$ kg^{-1})	T. N. (g kg^{-1})	Clay (g kg^{-1})
Sunchullí River						
Sediment (1) before discharge	6.34	0.226	11.58	4.18	1.18	40.84
Sediment (2) after discharge	4.85	1.181	16.55	2.99	0.91	52.82
Pelechuco River						
Sediment (1) before discharge	6.35	0.07	8.4	1.99	1.0	19.0
Sediment (2) after discharge	7.41	0.27	33.1	4.84	3.6	418.7
Turcos River						
Sedimento (1)	7.27	0.29	6.22	1.11	0.34	12.52
Rayo Rojo River						
Sedimento (1)	7.03	0.55	6.29	0.96	0.35	9.98

E.C.: Electrical conductivity; T.O.C.: total organic carbon; T.N.: total nitrogen; C.E.C.: cation exchange capacity.

pH of river sediments ranged from 4.85 (very strong acid-Sunchulli river) to 7.41 (sliglthy alkaline-Pelechuco river) (Soils Survey Division Staff, 1993) (Table 3). The sediments of all rives were not saline (Soils Survey Division Staff, 1993). CEC, TOC and TN concentrations of the river sediments were lowers than those reported from lagoon sediments.

Heavy Metals and Metalloids Content in Soil and Sediments

The Hg and As contents of the topsoil from the four profiles in Sunchulli-Viscachani area were 0.38, 2.58, 9.94, and 2.96 mg Hg kg^{-1}; and 6.85, 14.95, 18.49, 20.45 mg As kg^{-1}. In comparison, the concentrations in the subsoil (deepest horizon) were 0.09, 0.34, 1.27 and 0.23 mg Hg kg^{-1} and 9.24, 8.84, 8.67 and 11.03 mg As kg^{-1} (Table 4). These results suggest that atmospheric deposition of Hg and As could take places in this area for all the studied profiles; however some studies have shown that in many tropical areas Hg is frequently high in soils, likely as a result of the atmospheric deposition of Hg over thousands to perhaps millions of years (Lechler et al. 2000).

Possibly the observed values from profile I represent the natural accumulation of Hg and As in the topsoil. Oppositely, profile II, III and IV showed much higher concentration in the topsoil than subsoil, indicating active atmospheric deposition of Hg and As; therefore, for these profiles the Hg and As were originated from the atmospheric deposition and not from the bedrock. The Hg can be transported in small particles in the air and cause problems in the breathing system (Peñaloza and Reinhardt, 2000). These particles could reach the agricultural soils and pastures near to the mine areas by atmospheric transport.

Table 4. Metals and metallids concentrations in each horizon from Sunchulli-Viscachani, Katantika and Sural areas

Soil profiles	Lead (mg kg^{-1})	Copper (mg kg^{-1})	Zinc (mg kg^{-1})	Cadmium (mg kg^{-1})	Arsenic (mg kg^{-1})	Mercury (mg kg^{-1})
Sunchulli-Viscachani area						
Profile I - H1 (0-12 cm)	5.6	12.7	59.1	0.26	6.85	0.38
Profile I - H2 (12-24 cm)	4.2	9.4	66.5	0.01	9.24	0.09
Profile II – H (0-9 cm)	27.8	38.6	92.7	0.02	14.95	2.58
Profile II – Ah (9-24 cm)	9.3	29.1	100.4	2.43	9.96	0.05
Profile II – Bw (24-40 cm)	18.2	20.3	91.9	0.25	4.89	0.08
Profile II - C/R (>40 cm)	29.5	26.8	140.5	0.25	8.84	0.34
Profile III – Ah (0-11 cm)	23.8	17.4	84.3	2.84	18.49	9.94
Profile III - A/C (11-22 cm)	26.2	22.1	94.8	2.04	8.50	0.05
Profile III – C (22-40 cm)	37.1	32.4	82.8	0.01	8.67	1.27
Profile IV – Ah (0-12 cm)	33.1	23.0	81.7	1.68	20.45	2.96
Profile IV – C1 (12-32 cm)	35.8	24.9	101.9	1.00	16.07	1.97
Profile IV – 2C2 (32-54cm)	29.6	25.0	71.3	1.27	14.30	0.22
Profile IV – 2C3 (>54 cm)	24.5	27.0	71.1	2.04	11.03	0.23
Katantika area						
Profile I - Ah	15.6	17.7	140.3	1.88	10.99	0.08
Profile I - C	8.6	18.3	143.5	3.49	4.13	0.02
Sural area						
Profile I - A	18.3	19.6	145.7	4.66	5.53	0.06
Profile II - H	13.5	6.4	15.5	5.34	12.34	0.07

Analytical data (Table 4) shows that the concentrations of total metals, mainly Pb, Cu, and Zn, are higher in Profile II than in Profile I. Total Pb concentrations in surface horizons are 5.6 mg kg^{-1} in Profile I and 28 mg kg^{-1} in Profile II, likely this difference is due to natural occurrence of Pb. There is a tendency of Pb to concentrate in the felsic series of magmatic rocks and argillaceous sediments commonly reported to content Pb between 10 and 40 mg kg^{-1} (Kabata-Pendias and Pendias 2010). The concentration of Pb in C/R horizon in profile II is similar to Pb concentration in superficial horizon and supports our hypothesis that natural enrichment of metals in parent geological rocks can explain the differencc in metal contents between Profiles I and II. In addition, total Pb, Cu and Zn concentrations are similar in Profiles III and IV and show increase with depth for Pb and Cu (Table 4), indicating that geogenic origin is the main source for these metals.

Hg, As, Pb and Cu concentrations in the Katantica and Sural areas (Table 4) was lower than in the Sunchullí-Viscachani. Profiles samples showed values of Hg, As, Pb and Cu lower than the reference concentrations given by the used international regulation, therefore no Hg, As, Pb and Cu enrichment were observed in these profiles.

However, concentrations of Cd and Zn were higher than in Sunchulli-Viscachani area and largely exceed the thresholds levels, indicating a higher risk for human and environment, especially for Cd, though their origin must be geogenic since the highest concentrations were reported in subsoil.

Table 5. Metals and metallids concentrations in the sediments of Sunchulli, Viscachani, Katantika and Sural lagoons

Lagoon sediments	Lead ($mg\ kg^{-1}$)	Copper ($mg\ kg^{-1}$)	Zinc ($mg\ kg^{-1}$)	Cadmium ($mg\ kg^{-1}$)	Arsenic ($mg\ kg^{-1}$)	Mercury ($mg\ kg^{-1}$)
Sunchullí lagoon						
Sediment (1)	6.2	21.9	47.3	1.47	86.75	12.3
Sediment (2)	0.6	72.1	106.5	0.32	46.03	0.1
Sediment (3)	1.3	29.8	85.1	2.45	33.57	4.14
Viscachani lagoon						
Sediment (1)	38.6	27.3	39.9	0.93	10.64	11.7
Sediment (2)	23.9	19.5	99.3	2.52	16.93	23.7
Sural lagoon						
Sediment (1)	5.2	41.0	136.4	0.10	28.16	0.07
Sediment (2)	14.2	31.7	179.1	0.05	51.04	0.23
Katantika lagoon						
Sediment (1)	13.2	8.5	70.4	4.88	17.77	2.24
Sediment (2)	26.5	13.3	95.5	3.48	18.04	0.20

The Pb, Cu, Cd, Zn, Hg and As contents were varied in the Sunchullí and Viscachani lake sediments. According to the above mentioned regulatory most of the sediments could be classified as contaminated by Hg, As, Cd, Zn and Cu (Table 5). The Hg and As concentrations found in the lagoon sediments come likely from primitive amalgamation processes thought direct spill of waste to the water bodies. The highest concentration of Hg (23.7 mg kg^{-1}) was obtained in the sediment (2) of the Viscachani lagoon which is similar to the

Madeira river (Brazil) sediments concentration (19.83 mg kg^{-1}) (Pfeiffer et al. 1991). This sample was collected close to an area where the primitive amalgamation processes were carried out.

No enrichment was found for Pb, Cu and As in the sediments of Katantica lake, with concentrations lower than the levels proposed by the used regulations. However, sediment (1), located next to the mining operations, presented 2.24 mg Hg kg^{-1} and confirms that this lake exhibited an Hg enrichment (Table 5). In the same way, high concentrations of Zn and Cd were reported in both sediments collected in this lagoon, indicating that sediments are important sinks for these metals.

Hg, Pb and Cd concentrations in sediments of Sural lagoon did not reach high values (Table 5), all of them lower than the levels proposed by the used legislation. However, Zn, Cu and As concentrations exceeded those levels, indicating an enrichment of these elements in the sediments, and a potencial risk for the lagoon ecosystem.

Results showed that total Cu, Pb, As and Hg contents in sediments from the Sunchulli River come from mine direct discharges into the river. Total Pb and Hg contents in sediments collected before and after discharge points were 15,7 mg Pb kg^{-1}, 4.1 mg Hg kg^{-1} and 99 mg Pb kg^{-1}, 103 mg Hg kg^{-1}, respectively, confirming the significant Hg and Pb additions from mining activities in the study area (Table 6). These discharges of Pb and Hg (Cu and As) from mine operations can have significant medium and long-tern impacts on the environment. It should be mentioned that many settlement areas that are located in downstream zone consume water either for domestic or irrigation purposes, may therefore be subjected to significant health risks for using mine-impacted water from the Sunchulli River.

Table 6. Metals and metallids concentrations in the sediments of Sunchulli, Pelechuco, Turcos and Rayo Rojo rivers

River sediments	Lead	Copper	Zinc	Cadmium	Arsenic	Mercury
	(mg kg^{-1})	(mg kg^{-1})	(mg kg^{-1})	(mg kg^{-1})	(mg kg^{-1})	(mg kg^{-1})
Sunchullí River						
Sediment (1) before discharge	15.70	17.30	81.92	0.01	0.59	4.14
Sediment (2) after discharge	99.01	36.22	91.60	0.03	11.95	102
Pelechuco River						
Sediment (1) before discharge	3.24	12.66	119.48	0.01	14.66	0.08
Sediment (2) after discharge	2.28	22.14	121.53	0.04	52.26	6.85
Turcos River						
Sediment (1)	7.74	6.53	54.78	0.02	3.59	0.04
Rayo Rojo River						
Sediment (1)	20.81	15.28	36	0.02	53.95	8.55

In the case of the Pelechuco River, an increase of the Hg, As and Cu concentrations were reported in the sediments after discharge point compared with thc sample collected before that point (Table 6). This indicates that due to the cumulative contribution of the spills along the river, sediments of the lower basin have higher concentrations of Hg, As and Cu. Taking into account the allowed levels these sediments are mainly polluted by Hg and As.

Finally, in Rayo Rojo river sediments were reported higher concentrations of Pb, Cu, As and Hg than in the Turcos river, however only As and Hg exceeded the recommended level proposed by the used legislation.

CONCLUSSION

According with the results from soils profiles, Sunchulli-Viscachani mining area are polluted by As and Hg, likely associated with atmospheric deposition which, through direct inhalation and contact, can directly affect human health. In comparison to other polluted areas in the world, the Sunchulli-Viscachani mining area appears to be significantly affected and need to be studied further in greater detail. Oppositelly, concentrations of Cd and Zn largely exceed the thresholds levels in soils profiles collected from Katantika and Sural mining districts.

High contents of levels of Cu, Cd, As, Zn, and Hg were reported in Sunchulli and Viscachani Lake sediments, while Katantica lake showed high concentrations of Zn, Cd and Hg, and in the Sural lake were reported high levels of As, Zn and Cu. Results showed that Cu, Pb, As and Hg concentrations in sediments from the Sunchulli River; As, Hg and Cu in the Pelechuco River, and As and Hg in the Rayo Rojo River come from mine direct discharges into the rivers. These concentrations may cause a serious problem for aquatic life, related ecosystems and human health, in addition Hg methylation process could be occurring in sediment, which could pose high risk for the health of the environment.

Therefore, in order to reduce the human and ecological risk, there is an urgent need to study metals and metalloids availability and speciation in soils and sediments to better understand the cycling of these elements and transfer of metals/metalloids from soils into the food chain in the area.

REFERENCES

Alanoca. L., Maurice-Bourgoin. L. (2000). *Estudio de la contaminación por mercurio en la cuenca alta del Río Tuchi* (Study of mercury contamination in the upper basin of Rio Tuchi). La Paz, Bolivia.

Anne. P. (1945). Sur le dosage rapide du carbone organique des sols (The rapid assay of soil organic carbon). *Annales de Agronomie* (Annals of Agronomy). *2*. 162-172.

Honorato, R. (2000). *Manual de Edafología* (Handbook of Soil Science). Ediciones Universidad Católica de Chile Editions (Catholic University of Chile). Santiago, Chile.

Bower. C. A., Wilcox. L. V. (1965). Soluble salts. (In C. A. Black (ed.). *Methods on Soil Analysis* (933-940). Madison, Wisconsin, U.S.A. American Society of Agronomy.

BWRHABTGG (1995). *Besluit van de Vlaamse Regering Houdende Achtergrondwaarden*. Bodernsaneringsnomen en Toepassingen van Gereinigde Grond. Bruselas (Order of the Flemish Government Loving Background values. Bodernsaneringsnomen and Cleaned Ground Applications. Bruselas). Belgium. Ministry of Environment and Employment.

Campo. L. (2003). Componentes Programa Araucaria, resultados cartográficos (Components Araucaria program, mapping results) (pp 29-47). Programa Araucaria (Araucaria program).

Chapman. H. D. (1965). *Methods of Soil Analysis. Cation exchange capacity.* (In: C. A. Black (ed). (pp 891-900). Madison, Wisconsin, U.S.A. American Society of Agronomy.

Choong, T. S., Chuah, T. G., Robiah, Y., Gregory, F. L., Azni, I. (2007). Arsenic toxicity, health hazards and removal techniques from water: an overview. *Desalination. 217*. 139–166.

Cobertera. E. (1993). *Edafología aplicada: suelos, producción agraria, planificación territorial e impactos ambientales* (Applied soil science: soil, agricultural production, land use planning and environmental impacts). Ed Cátedra. Madrid. Spain.

Duchaufour. P. (1970). *Precis de Pedologie* (Just the Podologie) (481 pp). Masson. Paris.

Enríquez. J. C. (2001). *Minería, Minerales y Desarrollo Sustentable en Bolivia* (Mining, Minerals and Sustainable Development in Bolivia). La Paz. Bolivia. Servicios Ambientales (Environmental services).

FAO-ISRIC (2006). *Guidelines for Soil Description (revised)*, fourth ed. F.A.O, Roma. 97pp.

Faz. A., Martínez. S., Acosta. J. A., Millán. R., Vera. R., Sierrra. M.J., García. G., Muñoz. M. A. (2003) *Estudio sobre contaminación por actividades mineras en Apolobamba* (Study on pollution by mining activities in Apolobamba), pp 260. Internal report. Cartagena, Universidad Politécnica de Cartagena-Agencia Española de Cooperación Internacional-Programa Araucaria.

Guan, X., Du, J., Meng, X., Sun, Y., Sun, B., Hu, Q. (2012). Application of titanium dioxide in arsenic removal from water: a review. *Journal of Hazardous Materials. 215.* 1–16.

Horvat. M., Nolde. N., Fajon. V., Jereb. V., Logar. M., Lojen. S., Jacimovic. R., Falnoga. I., Faganeli. J., Drobne. D. (2003). Total mercury, methylmercury and selenium in mercury polluted areas in the province Guizhou, China. *Science of the Total Environment. 304.* 231–256.

Kabata-Pendias. A., Pendias. H. (2010). *Trace Elements in soils and plants*. Forth edition CRC Press, Boca Raton.

Lechler. P. J., Miller. J. R., Lacerda. L. D., Vinson. D., Bonzongo. J. C., Lyons. W. B., Warwick. J. J. (2000). Elevated mercury concentrations in soils, sediments, water, and fish of the Madeira River basin, Brazilian Amazon: a function of natural enrichments?. S *Science of the Total Environment. 260.* 87-96.

Lindquist. O., Rhode. H. (1985). Atmospheric Mercury—a review. *Tellus.* 136-157.

Litter. M. I., Morgada. M. E. (2010) Bundschuh, J. Possible treatments for arsenic removal in Latin American waters for human consumption. *Environmental Pollution. 158(5).* 1105-1118.

Loayza. F., Franco. I. (2000). *Estudio Ambiental, Socio Cultural y Económico de la Minería y la Comunidad en Bolivia, Perú y Chile. El Caso Boliviano* (Environmental, Socio-Cultural and Economic Survey of Mining and the Community in Bolivia, Peru and Chile. The Bolivian Case). Centro Internacional de Investigaciones para el Desarrollo, División Minería e Industria - Banco Mundial International (Centre for Development Research, Mining and Industry Division - World Bank), La Paz, Bolivia.

Malm. O., Pfeiffer. W. C., Souza. C.M.M., Reuther. R. (1990). Mercury pollution due to gold mining in the Madeira river basin. Brazil. *AMBIO. 19 (1).* 11-15.

Maurice-Bourgoin. L., Quiroga. I. (2001). *Total mercury distribution and importance of the biomagnification process in rivers of the Bolivian*

Amazon. In: The Ecohidrology of South America Rivers and Wetlands (McClain M., Ed.), IAHS Special Publication nº 6, pp 49-66.

Maurice-Bourgoin. L., Quiroga. I., Guyot. J. L., Malm. O. (1999). Mercury pollution in the upper Beni River basin. Bolivia. *AMBIO. 28 (4).* 302-306.

Mays. D. A., Bengtson. G. W. (1978). *Lime and fertilizer use in land reclamation in humid regions. In: Reclamation of drastically disturbed lands.* F. W. Schaller y P. Sutton, pp 742. Madison (eds.). American Society of Agronomy.

M.D.S.M.A. (Ministerio de Desarrollo Sostenible y Medio Ambiente - Bolivia) (1996). *Proyecto Piloto Oruro: Documento Plan de Gestión Ambiental* (Oruro Pilot Project: Environmental Management Plan Document). Swedish Geological AB, La Paz.

N.M.H.P.P.E. (1994). Netherlands Ministry of Housing. *Physical Planning and Environment.* Leidschendam. Holland.

Peech. M. (1965). *Methods or Soil Analisis. Hidrogen-ion activity.* (In C.A. Black (ed.). (pp 914-916) American Society of Agronomy. Madison, Wisconsin, U.S.A.

Peñaloza. Reinhardt. (2000). *Problemas ambientales de la minería Boliviana. Estudio de caso de la minería en el área de la ciudad de Potosí*, Proyecto IDRC – WRI – CIPMA: Identificando los Impactos Económicos y Ambientales de la Liberalización del Comercio: Una Aplicación al Sector Minero, Fundación MEDMIN (Identifying Economic and Environmental Impacts of Trade Liberalization: An Application to the Mining Sector Foundation MEDMIN).

Pfeiffer. W. C., Maim. O., Souza. C.M.M., Drude. L., Silveira. E. G., Bastos. W. R. (1991). Mercury in the Madeira River ecosystem, Rondonia, Brazil. *Ecologycal Management. 38.* 239-245.

Pfeiffer. W. C., Lacerda. L. D., Salomons. W., Malm. O. (1993). Environmental fate of mercury from gold-mining in the Brazilian Amazon. *Environmental Review.* 26-37.

Podwojewski. P., Poulenard. J., Nguyet. M.L., de Rouw. A., Nguyen. V. T., Pham. Q. H., Tran. D. T. (2011). Climate and vegetation determine soil organic matter status in an alpine inner-tropical saoil catena in the Fan Si Pan Mountain, Vietnam. *Catena. 87.* 226-239.

Risser. J. A., Baker. D. E. (1990) *Testing soils for toxic metals.* In: R. L. Westerman, pp 275-298 (Ed). Madison, Soil Testing and plant analysis. Soil Sci. Soc. Amer. Spec. Publ. 3. 3rd Ed.

Soil Survey Division Staff. (1993). *Soil Survey Manual.* USDA Handbook 18, U.S. Government Printing Office, Washington, DC. 435 pp.

Soil Survey Staff. (2006) *Keys to Soil Taxonomy,* 10th ed. Natural resources Conservation service (NRCS), Washington DC.

Travnikov. O. (2005). Contribution of the intercontinental atmospheric transport to mercury pollution in the Northern Hemisphere. Atmos. Environ. 39:7541–7548USDA (2003) National Soil Survey Handbook. Natural Resources Conservation service title 430-VI. Part 618. 47. Reaction (pH): Soil Properties and Qualities.

W.H.O. (WorldHealth Organization) (2014). Arsenic. http://www.who.int/mediacentre/factsheets/fs372/en/#.

W.R.B. (2006) *World Reference Base for Soil Resources 2006.* A framework for international classification, correlation and communication 103, pp 128. Rome.

Zang-Ho. S., Ki-Hyun. K., Min-Young. K., Meehye. L. (2005). Modeling study of reactive gaseous mercury in the urban air. *Atmospheric Environment. 39.* 749–761.

Zemmrich. A., Manthey. M., Zerbe. S., Oyunchimeg. D. (2010) Driving environmental factors and the role of grazing in grassland communities: A comparative study along an altitudinal gradient in Western Mongolia. *Journal of Arid Envionment. 74.* 1271-1280.

INDEX

#

A

B

C

D

E

J

K

L

M

N

O

P

Q

R

S

T